MICROSOFT WINDOWS 3.1

PUBLISHED BY

Microsoft Press
A Division of Microsoft Corporation
One Microsoft Way
Redmond, Washington 98052-6399

Library of Congress Cataloging-in-Publication Data
Nelson, Stephen L., 1959-
Field guide to Microsoft Windows 3.1/Stephen L. Nelson.
p. cm.
Includes index.
ISBN 1-55615-640-5
1. Windows (Computer programs). 2. Microsoft Windows (Computer File)
I. Title.
QA76.76.W56N4586 1994
005.4'3--dc20 93-48487
CIP

Printed and bound in the United States of America.

3 4 5 6 7 8 9 QEQE 9 8 7 5 6 4

Distributed to the book trade in Canada by Macmillan of Canada, a division of Canada Publishing Corporation.

A CIP catalogue record for this book is available from the British Library.

Microsoft Press books are available through booksellers and distributors worldwide. For further information about international editions, contact your local Microsoft Corporation office. Or contact Microsoft Press International directly at fax (206) 936-7329.

Acquisitions Editor: Lucinda Rowley

Project Editor: Tara Powers-Hausmann

Technical Contact: Mary DeJong

FIELD GUIDE TO

MICROSOFT WINDOWS 3.1

Stephen L. Nelson

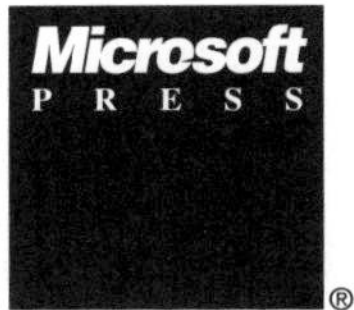

The Field Guide to Microsoft Windows 3.1 is divided into four sections. These sections are designed to help you find the information you need quickly.

1 ENVIRONMENT

Terms and ideas you'll want to know to get the most out of Windows. All the basic parts of Windows 3.1 are shown and explained. The emphasis here is on quick answers, but most topics are cross-referenced so that you can find out more if you want to.

Diagrams of key Windows components, with quick definitions, cross-referenced to more complete information.

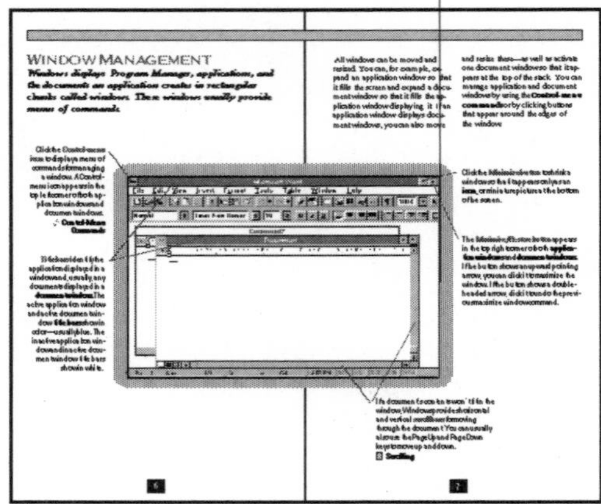

Tipmeister

Watch for me as you use this Field Guide. I'll point out helpful hints and let you know what to watch for.

INTRODUCTION

In the field and on expedition, you need practical solutions. Fast. This Field Guide provides just these sorts of lightning quick answers. But take two minutes and read the introduction. It explains how this unusual little book works.

How to Use This Book

Sometime during grade school, my parents gave me a field guide to North American birds. With its visual approach, its maps, and its numerous illustrations, that guide delivered hours of enjoyment. The book also helped me better understand and more fully appreciate the birds in my neighborhood. And the small book fit neatly in a child's rucksack. But I'm getting off the track.

What Is a Field Guide?

This book works in the same way as that field guide. It organizes information visually with numerous illustrations. And it does this in a way that helps you more easily understand and, yes, even enjoy working with Microsoft Windows. For new users, the Field Guide provides a visual path to the essential information necessary to start using Windows. But the Field Guide isn't only for beginners. For experienced users, the Field Guide provides concise, easy-to-find descriptions of Windows tasks, terms, and techniques.

When You Have a Question

Let me explain then how to find the information you need. You'll usually want to flip first to the first section, **Environment**, which is really a visual index. You find the picture that shows what you want to do or the task you have a question about. If you want to know how to work with some thingamajig on a dialog box, for example, you flip to pp. 8-9, which shows a dialog box.

Next you read the captions that describe the parts of the picture—or key elements of Windows. Say, for example, that you can't figure out how to select a dialog box button. The dialog box on pp. 8-9 includes captions that describe the parts of a dialog box. These key elements appear in **boldface** type to make them stand out.

When You Need More Information

You'll notice that some captions are followed by a little paw print and additional **boldface** terms. These refer to entries in the second section, Windows A to Z, and provide more information related to the caption's contents. (The paw print shows you how to track down the information you need. Get it?)

Windows A to Z is a dictionary of more than 150 entries that define terms and describe tasks. (After you've worked with Windows a bit or if you're already an experienced user, you'll often be able to turn directly to this section.) So, if you have just read the caption that says Windows provides online **Help**, you can flip to the Help entry in Windows A to Z.

Any time an entry in Windows A to Z appears as a term within an entry, I'll **boldface** it the first time it appears in the entry. For example, as part of describing how Help works, I might tell you that Help is a separate **application**. In this case, the word **application** will appear in bold letters—alerting you to the presence of an Application entry. If you don't understand the term or want to do a bit of brushing up, you can flip to the entry for more information.

When You Have a Problem

The third section, Troubleshooting, describes problems that new or casual users of Windows often encounter. Following each problem description, I list one or more solutions you can employ to fix the problem.

When You Wonder About a Command

The Quick Reference describes the Program Manager, File Manager, Print Manager, and Control Panel menu **commands**. If you want to know what a specific command does, turn to the Quick Reference. Don't forget about the Index either. You can look there to find all references in this book to any single topic.

Conventions Used Here

I have developed some conventions to make using this book easier for you. Rather than use wordy phrases, such as "Activate the File menu and then choose the Print command," to describe how you choose a command, I'm just going to say, "Choose the File Print command."

Another thing. Rather than describe in text how you find **program items** in **groups**, I'll just visually show you the path to an application. For example, if I'm talking about Windows **Terminal** accessory, I'll show this path:

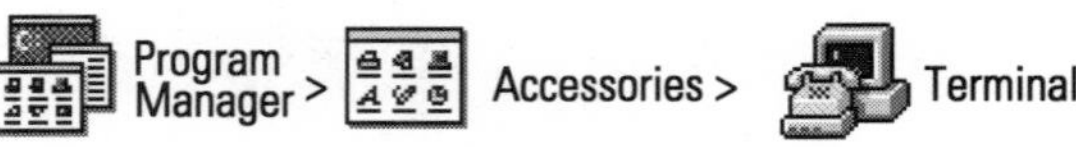

What this shows you is that you can start the Terminal accessory by displaying Program Manager, displaying the Accessories group, and then selecting the Terminal program item—for example, by double-clicking it.

ENVIRONMENT

Need to get the lay of the land quickly? Then the Environment is the place to start. It defines the key terms you'll need to know and the core ideas you should understand as you begin exploring Microsoft Windows.

WINDOWS PROGRAM MANAGER

Starting Microsoft Windows typically starts Program Manager. Program Manager organizes your Windows-based applications into groups. Program Manager can start applications automatically, or it can allow you to start any application manually (with commands).

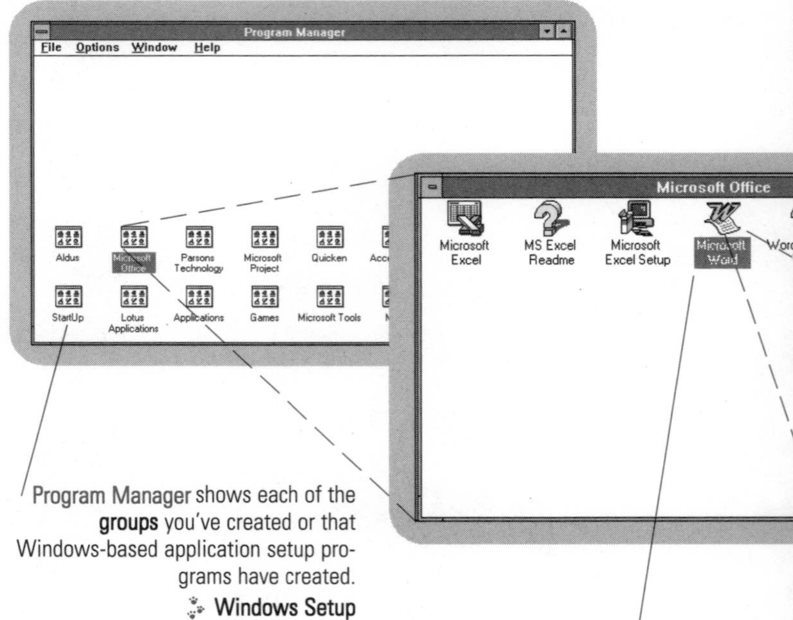

Program Manager shows each of the **groups** you've created or that Windows-based application setup programs have created.

Windows Setup

Program items identify **applications** and accessories. You start applications by double-clicking their program-item **icons**.

Starting Windows-Based Applications

To start a Windows-based application, you first start Windows. Then you display a **group** and double-click one of its **program items** (which can be an **application**, an **accessory,** or a **document**). Windows uses a picture, or **icon**, to represent each program item in a group. Examples of Windows-based programs include well-known applications such as Lotus 1-2-3, Microsoft Excel, Microsoft Word, and WordPerfect.

Windows comes with a large set of handy although less-powerful accessory applications, including Calculator, Calendar, a simple word processor named Write, and a telecommunications program called Terminal.

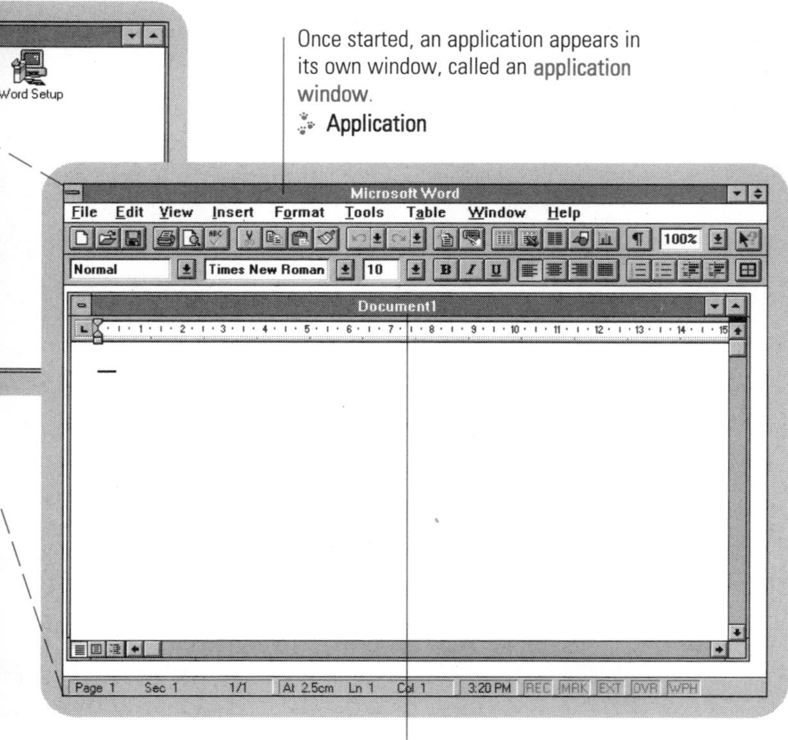

Once started, an application appears in its own window, called an application window.

Application

Applications typically display windows of their own—usually called document windows.

WINDOWS FILE MANAGER

Windows isn't just a platform useful for starting applications. It also includes applications—such as File Manager shown below—for managing files, disks, and printers.

File-menu commands let you manage application and document files.

Copying Files; Erasing Files; Moving Files; Renaming Files; Unerasing Files

Disk-menu commands let you copy, format, and name floppy disks.

Formatting Floppies

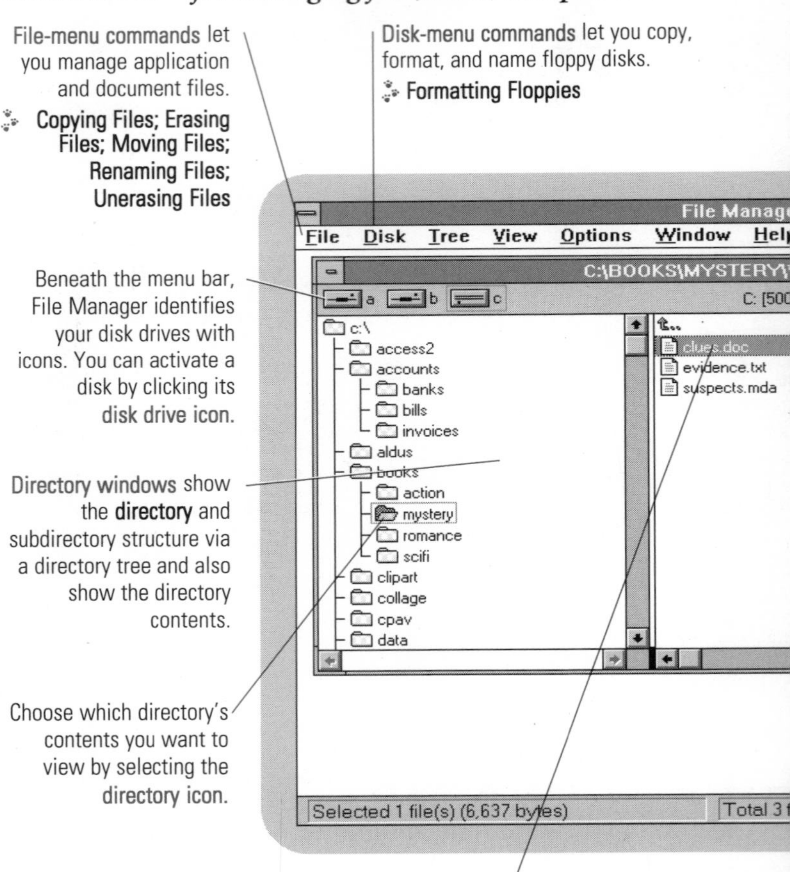

Beneath the menu bar, File Manager identifies your disk drives with icons. You can activate a disk by clicking its disk drive icon.

Directory windows show the **directory** and subdirectory structure via a directory tree and also show the directory contents.

Choose which directory's contents you want to view by selecting the directory icon.

Select files and directories by clicking them with the mouse or by using the Tab and direction keys.

File Manager

The Windows File Manager application, for example, lets you easily work with files and disks. You can copy and move files and directories by clicking and dragging the mouse, for example. And you can easily delete (and often undelete) files and format disks by choosing menu commands.

File Manager isn't alone

File Manager isn't the only system management tool provided by Windows. Windows also comes with Print Manager, which manages your printers, and Control Panel, which manages an assortment of system settings and devices.

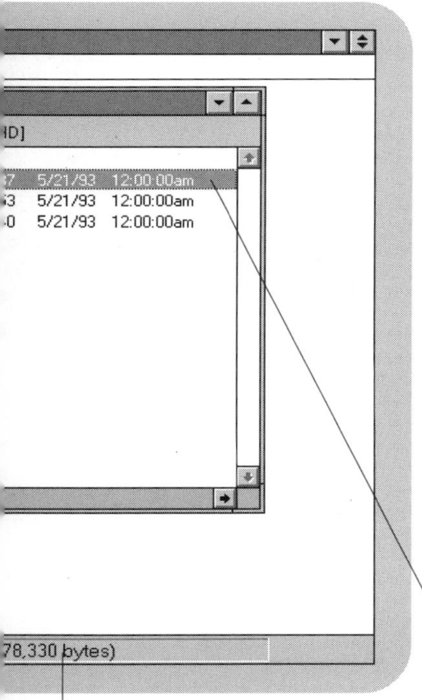

Start applications from **File Manager** by double-clicking the application files. You can also start an application and open a document by double-clicking document files.

Associating Files

The File Manager status bar provides information about the selected file, directory, and disk. You can tell how much free space your hard disk has by clicking its disk drive icon and selecting the **root directory.**

WINDOW MANAGEMENT

Windows displays Program Manager, applications, and the documents an application creates in rectangular chunks called windows. These windows usually provide menus of commands.

Click the Control-menu box to display a menu of commands for managing a window. A Control-menu box appears in the top left corners of both application windows and document windows.

Control-Menu Commands

Title bars identify the application displayed in a window and, usually, any documents displayed in a **document window.** The active application window and active document window title bars appear in color—usually blue. The inactive application window and inactive document window title bars appear in white.

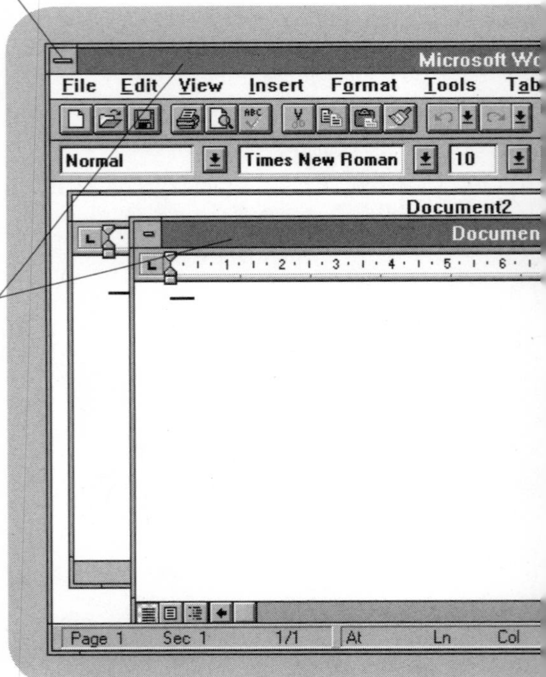

All windows can be moved and resized. You can, for example, expand an application window so that it fills the screen and expand a document window so that it fills the application window displaying it. If an application window displays document windows, you can also move and resize these—as well as activate one document window so that it appears at the top of the stack. You can manage application and document windows by using the **Control-menu commands** or by clicking buttons that appear around the edges of the window.

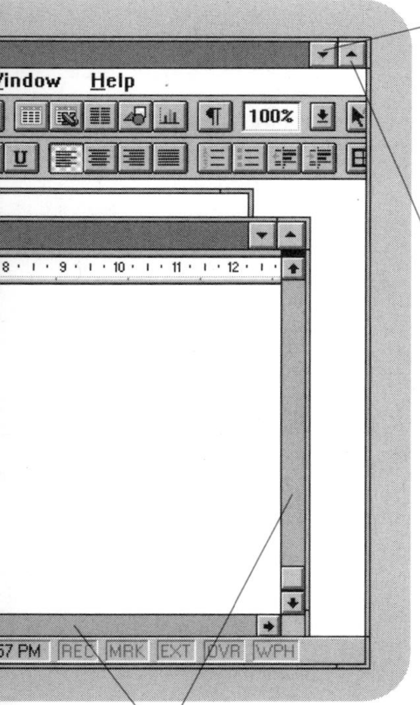

Click the Minimize button to shrink a window so that it appears only as an **icon,** or miniature picture, at the bottom of the screen.

The Maximize/Restore button appears in the top right corners of both **application windows** and **document windows.** If the button shows an upward pointing arrow, you can click it to maximize the window. If the button shows a double-headed arrow, click it to undo the previous maximize window command.

If a document's contents won't fit in the window, Windows provides horizontal and vertical scroll bars for moving through the document. You can usually also use the PageUp and PageDown keys to move up and down.

Scrolling

MENUS AND COMMANDS

Windows and Windows-based application menus and commands work in the same basic way. To easily use Windows and Windows-based applications, then, you'll want to learn the mechanics of the Windows menus and commands.

Beneath an application window's title bar, you'll usually see a **menu bar**. It organizes the commands into related sets.

Toolbars

Activate a **menu** by clicking it with the mouse. When you do, Windows displays the menu's commands.

Windows identifies those **commands** that display dialog boxes by following the command names with ellipses (...). If a command doesn't make sense in a given situation, Windows disables it. Windows identifies these disabled commands by displaying their names in gray letters.

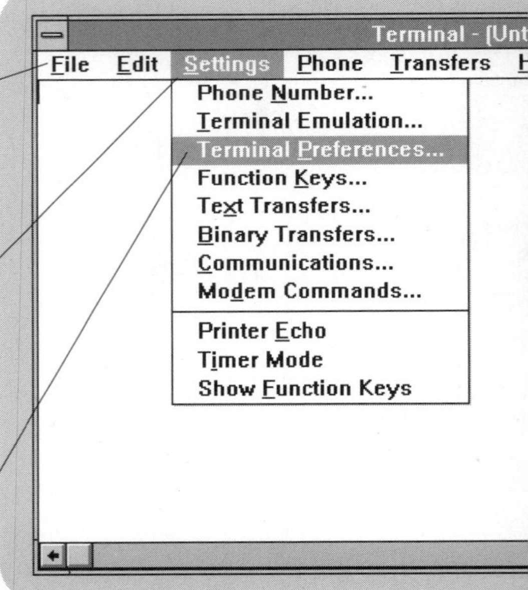

Check boxes are on-off switches. You turn on and turn off a check box by clicking it. Windows and Windows-based applications show an X if the box is turned on.

When you want a Windows-based application to do something, you issue a command by activating a menu, or list of commands, and then choosing one of the commands. If the Windows-based application needs more information from you to carry out the command, it displays a **dialog box.** Dialog boxes use buttons and boxes to collect this information.

Help is the rightmost menu in most Windows-based applications. It lists commands for starting Windows online Help.

Using the keyboard

It's easiest to select elements in Windows by clicking the mouse. You can also use the keyboard. To do this, you press Alt and then the underlined letter shown in the item you want to select. You can press Alt and then the letter F to activate the File menu, for example. You can press Alt and the letter W to select the Line Wrap check box in the top left corner of the dialog box shown here.

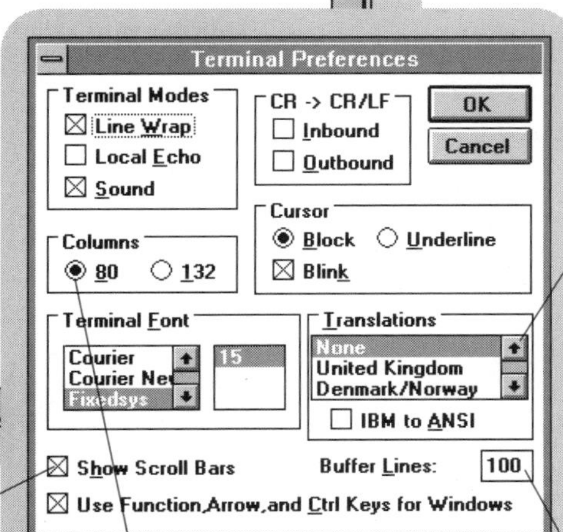

List boxes give a limited set of choices. To make your choice, click the list box and then click the list entry. If a list won't fit in a box, Windows displays a **scroll bar** for moving through the list.

Drop-Down List Boxes

Option buttons are mutually exclusive sets of choices. You mark your choice by clicking a button. Windows or an application shows your choice by inserting a bullet in the button.

Text boxes are input blanks you fill in. To use one, you click the text box and begin typing.

MULTITASKING IN WINDOWS

Windows has the ability to run more than one application at a time. In other words, Windows is a multitasking operating environment.

You start applications with **Program Manager**. If Program Manager isn't displayed, display **Task List**—for example, by pressing Ctrl+Esc. Then select Program Manager.

The **background applications'** windows usually won't show unless your foreground application window is smaller than the screen. If the background applications' windows show, their title bars are usually a color different from the color of the active application's title bar.

The **foreground application** is the one whose window is in front of all other windows on your screen. If more than one application window shows, you can tell which application is in the foreground by looking at its title bar. The foreground application's title bar shows in color—usually blue.

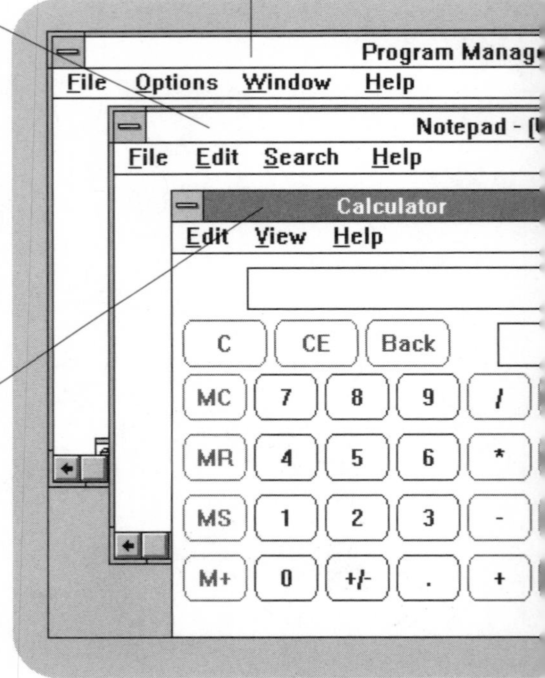

Multitasking isn't difficult—even if you're new to Windows. In fact, you probably already multitask—even though you don't realize it. For example, when you tell your word processor to print, Windows starts another **application** called Print Manager. It's this other application that does the work of actually printing.

The advantages of multitasking may be apparent to you. If your work requires both a word processor and a spreadsheet program, you can run both these applications simultaneously—and you can easily flip back and forth between them. Multitasking also makes it easy to share data between applications using the Windows **Clipboard**.

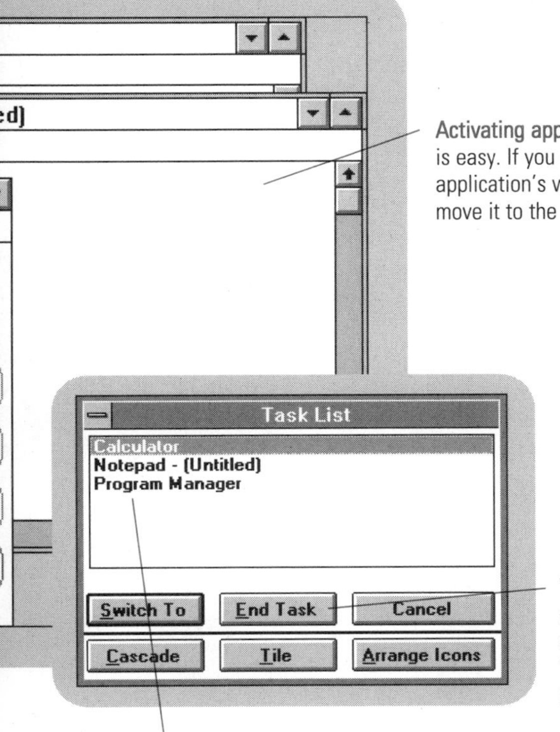

Activating applications with the mouse is easy. If you can see a background application's window, you can click it to move it to the foreground.

You can use the End Task command button to stop an application. But beware! You need to save your work before quitting.

Task List shows **Program Manager** and any applications that are currently running. You can change which application runs in the foreground by selecting its name and then clicking the Switch To command button. You can also double-click an application's name.

WINDOWS A TO Z

Maybe it's not a jungle out there. But you'll still want to keep a survival kit close at hand. Windows A to Z, which starts on the next page, is just such a survival kit. It lists in alphabetic order the tools, terms, and techniques you'll need to know.

386 Enhanced Mode → Mode

Accessories Windows comes with a bunch of mini-applications like **Calculator, Cardfile,** and **Write.** These babies are called accessories by some. Windows stores them in the Accessories group.

Active Document The active **document** is the one you can see in front of any other documents in an **application window**. It's also the document upon which selected commands act.

In a word processor application, you'll see the thing you're writing—a report, for example—in a **document window**. In a spreadsheet application, you'll see the spreadsheet you're creating in a document window. Many, perhaps most, applications let you display more than one document window in the application window.

Changing the active document

You can flip-flop between open documents—if you've got more than one open—by choosing one of the numbered menu commands from the Window menu. Each numbered command names an open document window. You can also press Ctrl+F6 or Ctrl+Tab to move to the next document window.

Active and Inactive Windows The active **document window** is the one you see in front of any other document windows in the **application window**. Any commands you choose affect the document in the active document window.

The active application window—such as the Microsoft Word application window—is the one that appears in front of any other application windows on your screen. (Cleverly, this is called the foreground. The inactive application windows, if there are inactive applications, appear in the background.)

Activating Application Windows

You can activate a different application window by clicking the window or by choosing the Switch To command from the Control menu.

Activating Document Windows

You can activate a different document window by clicking the window or by choosing the Window menu command that names the window.

ANSI Characters The ANSI character set includes all the ASCII characters your keyboard shows plus the special characters your keyboard doesn't show, such as the Japanese yen symbol, ¥, or the British pound symbol, £. Even though these special characters don't appear on your keyboard, you can still use them in most Windows-based applications. You can, for example, enter ANSI characters into word processor documents. And you can enter an ANSI character into most **text boxes**.

continues

ANSI Characters *(continued)*

Adding ANSI Characters

To enter an ANSI character, position the **insertion point** where you want the character, hold down Alt, and then, using the numeric keypad, enter the ANSI code for that character. For example, the ANSI character code for the Japanese yen symbol is 0165. To enter a yen symbol into a document, hold down Alt and type *0165* using the numeric keypad. Be sure to include the zero. (Refer to the Windows user documentation for a list of ANSI character codes.)

Removing ANSI Characters

To delete an ANSI character, select it and press Del, or backspace over the character.

Anti-Virus

MS-DOS version 6 or later comes with Microsoft Anti-Virus, a utility that attempts to safeguard your personal computer from computer **viruses.** If Windows version 3.1 and MS-DOS version 6 or later came with your personal computer, you may be able to use the Microsoft Anti-Virus from inside Windows.

Starting the Anti-Virus Utility

You start the Anti-Virus utility in one of two ways. (Which way you start depends on how you installed MS-DOS version 6.) You may be able to start **File Manager** and choose the Tools Antivirus command.

 Program Manager >  Main >  File Manager

Or you may be able to use the Anti-Virus **program item** in the Microsoft Tools **group.**

 Program Manager >  Microsoft Tools >  Anti-Virus

Using the Anti-Virus Utility

To search for and then destroy any viruses that have infected your computer's disks, follow these steps once you've started the Anti-Virus utility:

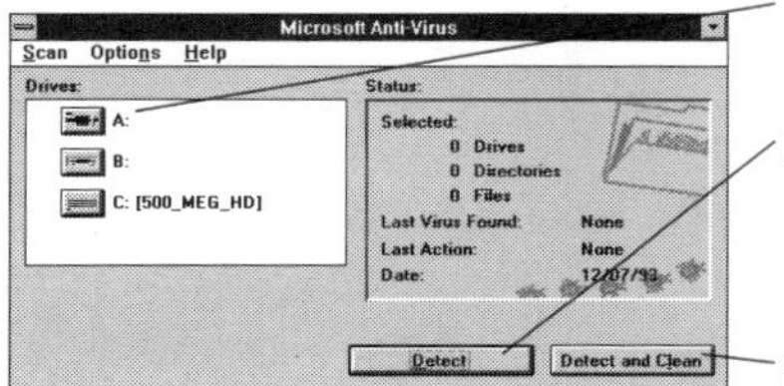

1. Click the disk you want to search.
2. Click Detect to simply search for viruses in memory and on the selected disk.
3. Click Detect and Clean to search and destroy viruses in memory and on disk.

Listing the Viruses That Anti-Virus Can Find

Choose the Scan Virus List command to display a list of the viruses that the Anti-Virus utility can locate and eradicate.

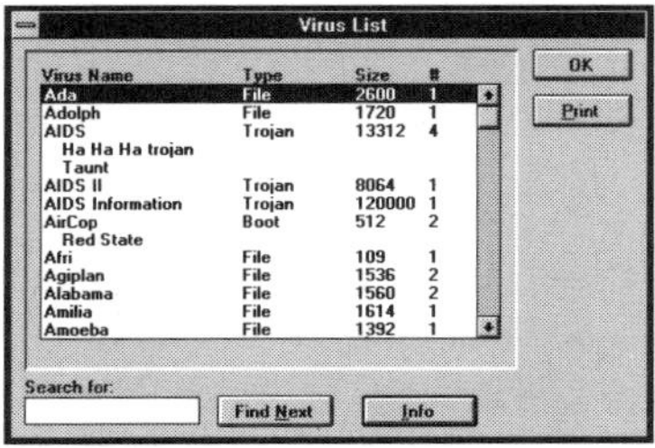

Virus Name	Type	Size	#
Ada	File	2600	1
Adolph	File	1720	1
AIDS	Trojan	13312	4
Ha Ha Ha trojan			
Taunt			
AIDS II	Trojan	8064	1
AIDS Information	Trojan	120000	1
AirCop	Boot	512	2
Red State			
Afri	File	109	1
Agiplan	File	1536	2
Alabama	File	1560	2
Amilia	File	1614	1
Amoeba	File	1392	1

Scroll through the list box to see which viruses Anti-Virus can find. Click Info to get more information about the selected virus.

Application Applications are the programs you buy down at the software store or through the mail to do work—work such as word processing, spreadsheeting, databasing, accounting, and a bunch of other tasks.

Microsoft sells several well-known and very popular applications, including Microsoft Access (a database program), Microsoft Excel (a spreadsheet program), and Microsoft Word (a word processor). There are lots of other popular and well-known applications too: WordPerfect, Lotus 1-2-3, and Quicken are just three.

Exiting Windows-Based Applications; Starting Windows-Based Applications

---

Application Errors Sometimes an **application** asks Windows to do the impossible. When this happens, Windows displays a **message box** that alerts you to an application error. If you've got **Dr. Watson** running in the background, Dr. Watson also displays a window asking about the events leading up to the error.

Application Window The application window is the rectangle in which an **application** such as Lotus 1-2-3, Microsoft Excel, Microsoft Word, or WordPerfect displays its **menu bar**, **toolbars**, and any open **document windows**.

ASCII Text Files An ASCII text file is simply a file that uses only the characters your keyboard shows. You can usually import an ASCII text file into a spreadsheet and word processor **application** using the application's File Open command.

Sharing data among applications

A last resort method for sharing data among applications is to create an ASCII text file. This works because many applications—spreadsheet, database, and accounting among others—produce text files.

Copying Data; Moving Data; Opening Files

Associating Files You can tell Windows which document files go with which **applications.** By doing this, you can start applications from **File Manager** simply by double-clicking an associated document file.

Starting File Manager

To start File Manager, display the Main **group** and double-click the File Manager **program item**.

 Program Manager >  Main >  File Manager

continues

Associating Files *(continued)*

Creating an Association

To create an association, follow these steps:

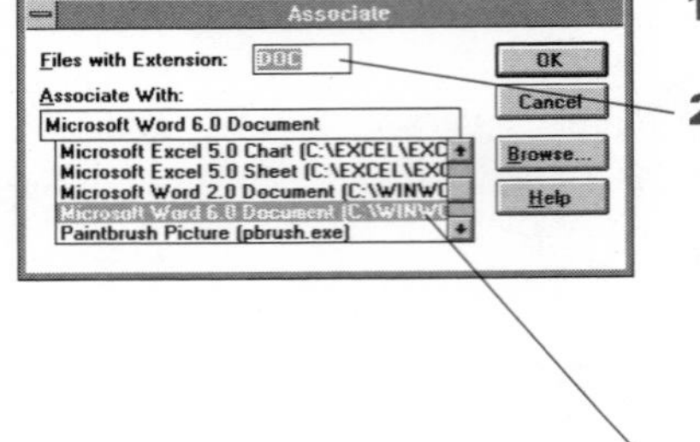

1. Choose the File Associate command.
2. Identify the file type by entering the file extension (the last three characters of the filename) you want to associate with a particular Windows-based application.
3. Select the Windows-based application from the Associate With list box.
4. Choose OK.

Starting an Application with an Associated File

To start the application you've associated with a particular file type, follow these steps:

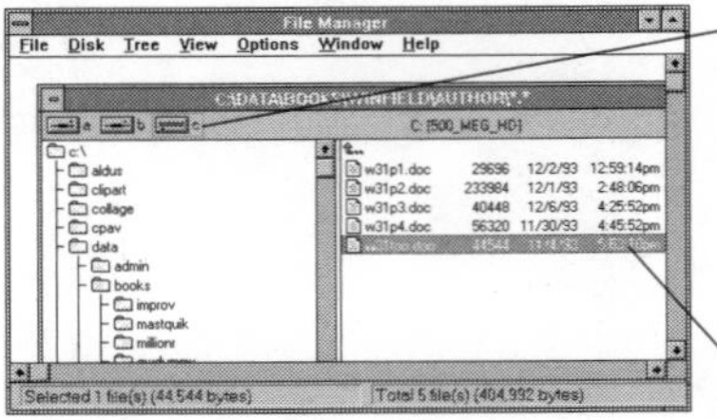

1. Click the disk that contains the file.
2. Click the directory and, if necessary, the subdirectory that contain the file.
3. Double-click the file. (File Manager starts the application you've associated and tells it to open the double-clicked file.)

Printing an Associated File

You can print an associated file from File Manager by selecting the file and choosing the File Print command. If the Print Manager minimized window icon shows on the desktop, you can also select the file and drag it to the Print Manager icon.

Background Applications Windows lets you run more than one application at a time. One of your applications runs in the foreground, meaning that it is the application which your commands affect and the application with the most or only visible window.

The other applications run in the background. Background applications' windows often aren't visible. You can't issue commands to a background application unless you first make it active, or move it to the foreground.

People sometimes refer to background applications as "inactive applications" because they appear in what Windows terms *inactive windows*. This isn't a very good description, however. A so-called inactive application may still be working, albeit very slowly.

Foreground Applications; Switching Tasks

Background application messages

When a background application wants to display a message, its title bar or icon may flash, alerting you to the message. Microsoft Excel, for example, includes an AutoSave feature that prompts you via a message box to save the open file every so often. If you've moved Excel to the background, it can't display the message that asks about the AutoSave. So Excel flashes its application window title bar or icon.

Backing Up The easiest way to back up (make a copy of) a single file or even a handful of files is to copy them to a floppy disk. If you want to make things slightly easier and you've got a handful of small files that can fit on a floppy disk or two, you may also be able to use the Backup utility if you're running MS-DOS version 6 or later.

Starting the Backup Utility

You can start the Backup utility in one of two ways. (Which way you start depends on how you installed MS-DOS version 6.) You may be able to start **File Manager** and choose the Tools Backup command.

 Program Manager >  Main >  File Manager

Or you may be able to use the Backup **program item** in the Microsoft Tools **group**.

 Program Manager >  Microsoft Tools >  Backup

I need to point out here, however, that if you've got a lot of stuff to back up—like the entire contents of a 200 megabyte hard disk, say—you'll want to back up to a tape. And for that you'll need to use a third-party Windows backup or MS-DOS backup utility.

Copying Files

Bit Map A bit map is simply a pattern of colored dots. On your screen, each colored dot is created as a pixel of light and is described by one or more bits (binary digits). This sounds like a bunch of gobbledygook, but if the pattern arranges the colored dots in the right way, you get a picture.

As a point of historical reference, I'll also mention that probably the best-known bit maps were those created in the late nineteenth century by the French impressionist painter Seurat. In this case, however, the colored dots were created by brushstrokes on canvas rather than by pixels of light. And you thought this book was just about computers.

Calculator

Use the Calculator **accessory** to make quick calculations.

Starting the Calculator

Start Calculator by displaying the Accessories **group** and then double-clicking the Calculator **program item**.

Program Manager > Accessories >

Calculator

Using the Calculator

Calculator in Windows works pretty much like a regular, handheld calculator.

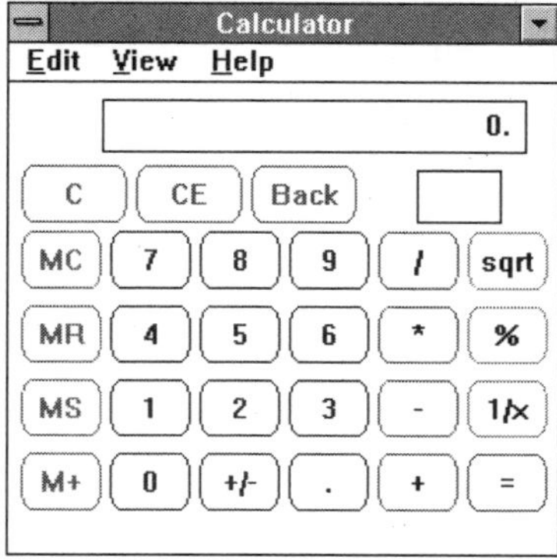

continues

Calculator *(continued)*

If you've got a mouse, you can click the calculator keys to enter the numbers and the operators. The calculator keys work like command buttons. Here are some example calculations.

Buttons you click	Result
3-2=	1
1+1=	2
5-2=	3
2*2=	4
10/2=	5
36sqrt	6

Clearing and Erasing Calculator Inputs

You use the C key to clear the numbers and operators you entered, the CE key to clear the last number you entered, and the Back key to clear the last digit you entered. For example, if you've just entered the numbers and operators 10+25, here's what the C, CE, and Back keys do:

Key	What it does
C	Erases all the numbers and operators you typed—in this case, 10+25
CE	Erases only the last number you typed, 25
Back	Erases only the last digit you typed, 5

Using the Percent Key

The calculator's % key lets you add, subtract, divide, and multiply a number by a percent. Here are some example calculations

Buttons you click	Result	What happens
10+50%=	15	Adds 50% of the value 10 to 10
10-50%=	5	Subtracts 50% of the value 10 from 10
10*50%=	50	Multiplies the value 10 by 50% of the value 10
10/50%=	2	Divides the value 10 by 50% of the value 10

Using the Inverse Key

The calculator's 1/x, or Inverse, key divides 1 by the entered value. If you enter 7 1/x=, Calculator returns 0.1428571428571 because 1/7 equals 0.1428571428571. If you click 1/x while this value shows on the calculator display, Calculator returns 7 because 1/0.1428571428571 equals 7.

Working with Memory

Calculator includes a memory feature too. Click the MS key to store the displayed value in **memory**. When you do, Calculator sticks a letter "M" in the box beneath the calculator display. Click M+ to add the displayed value to whatever is already stored in memory. Click MC to erase the value stored in memory. Click MR to retrieve the value stored in memory.

Copying and Pasting Values

Calculator's Edit Copy and Edit Paste commands let you move values to and from the Clipboard. Choose Edit Copy to move the value on the calculator display to the Clipboard. Choose Edit Paste to move the value on the Clipboard to the calculator display. Note that you can use the Edit Copy and Edit Paste commands to move values from Calculator to other Windows-based applications.

continues

Calculator *(continued)*

Using the Scientific Calculator

Calculator's View menu displays two commands, Scientific and Standard. They let you switch between the calculator shown earlier and a special version of the calculator that has keys for performing mathematical, trigonometric, and logarithmic operations.

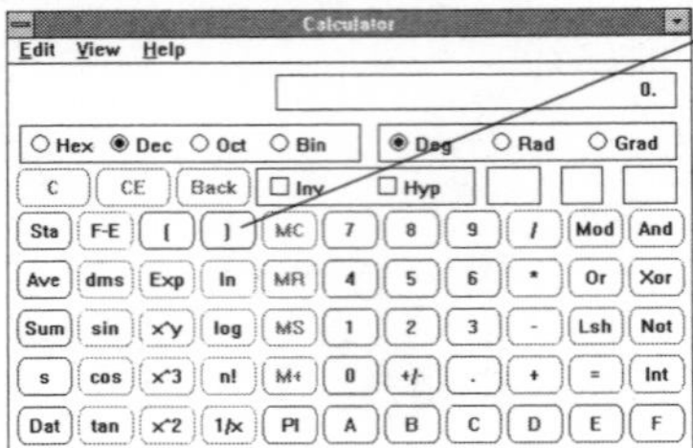

Use the parenthesis keys for performing calculations in some order other than the order you enter the operators.

Calendar

Windows comes with the Calendar **accessory,** which you can use to keep track of your business appointments, dinner parties, and the nights your bowling league meets.

Starting Calendar

Start Calendar by displaying the Accessories **group** and then double-clicking the Calendar **program item**.

 Program Manager >  Accessories >  Calendar

Entering Appointments

Once the Calendar window shows, you enter your appointments into the schedule slots.

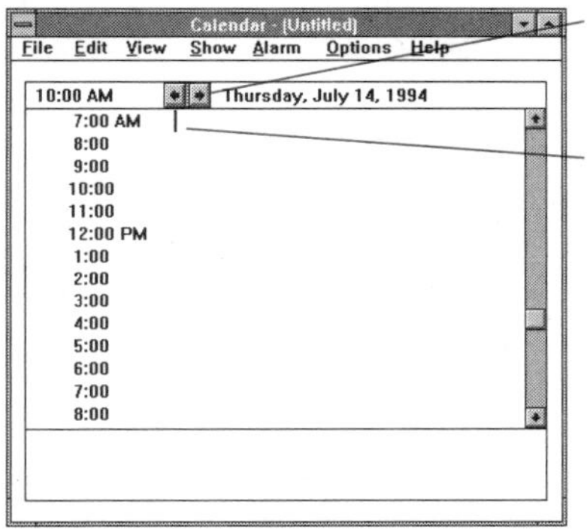

Use these buttons to move back and ahead one day at a time.

To enter an appointment, move the insertion point to the schedule slot and then type a blurb.

Use the View menu commands or the F8 and F9 keys to toggle between the day view of the calendar (shown here) and the month view of the calendar.

Saving an Appointment Calendar the First Time

To save your calendar to disk, follow these steps:

1. Choose the File Save As command.
2. Enter a filename for the calendar. You don't enter a file extension. Calendar supplies the correct file extension for you, CAL.
3. Use the Directories and Drives list boxes to specify where the Calendar file should be located.
4. Choose OK.

Retrieving an Appointment Calendar

To retrieve a calendar you've previously stored on disk, start Calendar and then follow these steps:

1. Choose the File Open command.
2. Enter the Calendar file's filename.
3. If necessary, use the Directories and Drives list boxes to specify where the Calendar file is located.
4. Choose OK.

continues

Calendar *(continued)*

Using an Appointment Alarm

Ever get to meetings late because you've been busily working away at your computer? No problem. You can tell Calendar to sound your computer's beeper as a reminder at the appointed hour—or a few minutes before.

To do this, enter the appointment as described earlier. Then select the appointment and follow these steps:

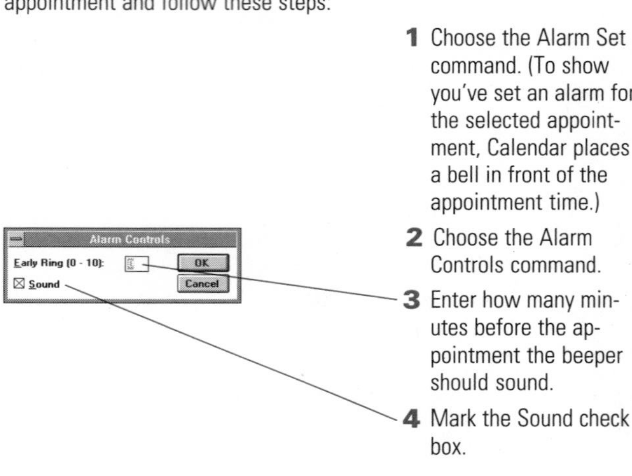

1. Choose the Alarm Set command. (To show you've set an alarm for the selected appointment, Calendar places a bell in front of the appointment time.)
2. Choose the Alarm Controls command.
3. Enter how many minutes before the appointment the beeper should sound.
4. Mark the Sound check box.

Printing Calendar

Choose the File Print command to print your appointment calendar. You can use the Print dialog box that Calendar displays to specify a range of dates.

Changing Calendar's Schedule

Calendar shows schedule slots every hour. You can change this by choosing the Options Day Settings command.

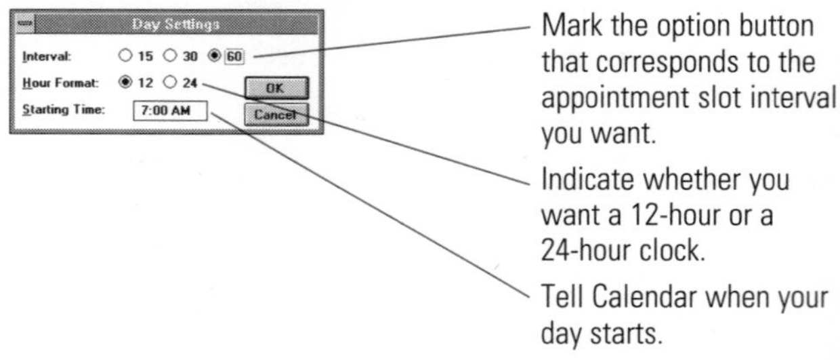

Mark the option button that corresponds to the appointment slot interval you want.

Indicate whether you want a 12-hour or a 24-hour clock.

Tell Calendar when your day starts.

Entering Appointment Times into the Calendar

If you want to schedule an appointment for a time that doesn't show, choose the Options Special Time command.

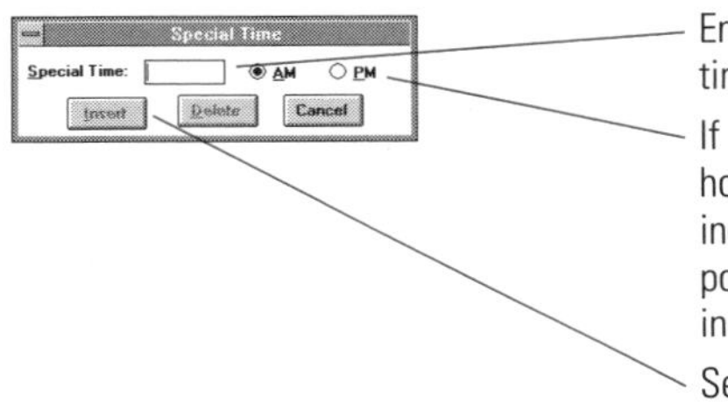

Enter the appointment time.

If the calendar uses a 12-hour clock, you'll need to indicate whether the appointment is in the morning or the afternoon.

Select Insert to add the appointment time.

Dates and Times; Opening Files; Saving Files

Cardfile

The Cardfile **accessory** lets you keep a names-and-addresses file on your computer.

Starting Cardfile

Start Cardfile by displaying the Accessories **group** and then double-clicking the Cardfile **program item.**

 Accessories >  Cardfile

continues

Cardfile *(continued)*

Adding Cardfile Entries

To add a name and address to Cardfile, follow these steps:

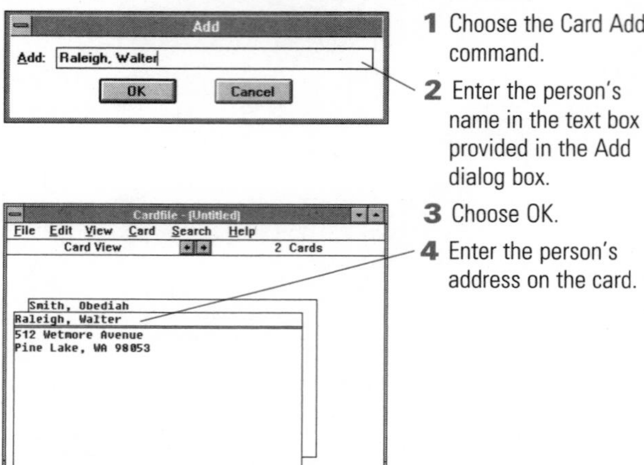

1 Choose the Card Add command.

2 Enter the person's name in the text box provided in the Add dialog box.

3 Choose OK.

4 Enter the person's address on the card.

Finding a Cardfile Entry

To find a name or an address in Cardfile, you can page back and forth using the PageUp and PageDown keys.

You can also display Cardfile entries in a list by choosing the View List command and scrolling through the list using the PageUp and PageDown keys.

You can also use the Search menu commands. If you know the person's name, choose the Search Go To command and then, when Cardfile displays the Go To dialog box, enter enough of the person's name to identify her or him and press Enter.

Printing Cardfile

Choose the File Print command to print the name and address card shown on the face of the Cardfile **application window.** Or choose the File Print All command to print a list of the names and addresses in your Cardfile.

Deleting Cardfile Entries

To remove a name and an address from Cardfile, display the card. Then choose the Card Delete command.

Saving a Cardfile File

To save your Cardfile file to disk, follow these steps:

1. Choose the File Save As command.
2. Enter a filename for your Cardfile file. You don't enter a file extension. Cardfile supplies the correct file extension for you, CRD.
3. Use the Directories and Drives list boxes to specify where the file should be located.
4. Choose OK.

Retrieving a Cardfile File

To retrieve a Cardfile file you've previously stored on disk, start Cardfile and then follow these steps:

1. Choose the File Open command.
2. Enter the Cardfile file's filename.
3. If necessary, use the Directories and Drives list boxes to specify where the file is located.
4. Choose OK.

Character Map

The Character Map **accessory** lets you easily add characters that don't appear on your keyboard to **documents.** For example, if you want to add one of the following Wingdings characters, or symbols, to a document, the easiest and only practical way is to use Character Map.

continues

Character Map *(continued)*

Starting Character Map

Start Character Map by displaying the Accessories **group** and then double-clicking the Character Map **program item.**

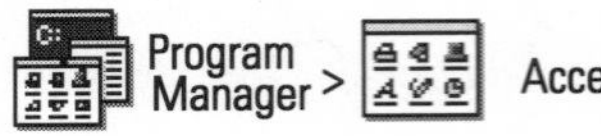

Accessories >

Using Character Map

To use Character Map, follow these steps:

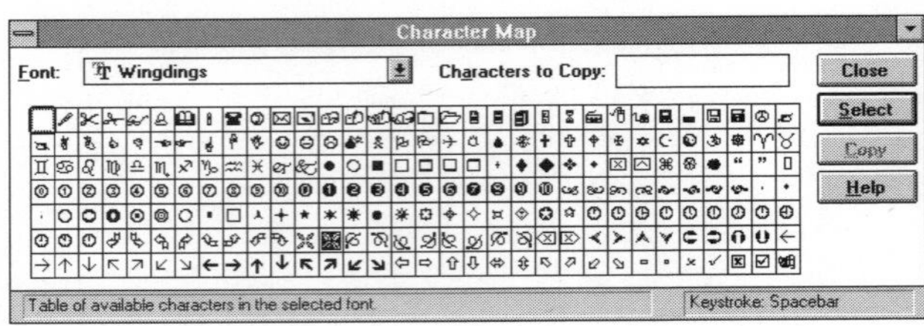

1. Activate the Font drop-down list box and select the font with the character you want. (If you want to enlarge the symbol after you add it, you'll find that scalable fonts such as TrueType or PostScript fonts work best.)
2. Find the character you want. If you can't see the character very well—and I never can—click the character box and hold down the mouse button. Character Map displays a pop-up box showing an enlarged version of the character.
3. Select the Select command button. Character Map places the selected character into the Characters to Copy text box.
4. Optionally, repeat steps 2 and 3 to add more characters to the Characters to Copy text box.
5. Select the Copy command button. (This copies the selected characters to the Clipboard.)
6. Switch to the application containing the document into which you want to place the special characters, position the insertion point, and then choose the application's Edit Paste command.

 **Fonts**

Check Boxes Check boxes are on-off switches. They often look like little squares. If the check box is turned off, the little square is empty. If the check box is turned on, the little square shows an **x**.

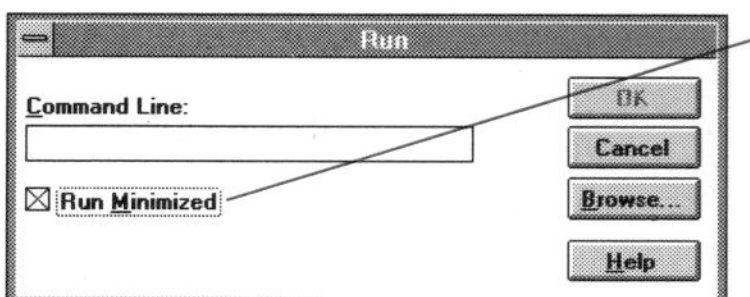

Windows uses X's to mark check boxes—as do many Windows-based applications.

To turn on and off a check box, you can click the box.

You can also use the keyboard. For example, you can use the Tab key to select the check box and then press the Spacebar to turn on and off the check box. Or, if the check box shows an underlined letter, you can also turn it on and off by pressing the Alt key and then the underlined letter. For example, you can turn on and off the Run Minimized check box in the preceding figure by pressing Alt+M.

Click

Click is a shortcut description for this two-step sequence:

1. You move the mouse pointer so that it rests over some object—such as a **menu** name.
2. You press and release the left mouse button. (It'll probably make a clicking sound as you do this.)

Rather than describe this two-step sequence half a billion times in a user guide, writers refer to the process as clicking the object. If you move the mouse pointer over a menu name and press and release the left mouse button, for example, you say you clicked the menu name.

Double-Click; Drag

Clip Art

Clip art refers to the pictures that you can paste into **documents**. Many word processors and drawing packages come with clip art images.

This clip art image comes with Microsoft Word for Windows version 6.

Clipboard Ever see the television show "Star Trek"? If you did, you may remember the transporter room. It let the *Starship Enterprise* move Captain Kirk, Mr. Spock, and just about anything else just about anywhere. The Clipboard is the Windows equivalent of the *Enterprise*'s transporter room. With the Clipboard, Windows easily moves just about anything anywhere. When working with a Windows-based application, you can use the Clipboard to move chunks of text, tables, and even graphic images to and from different files. You can also use the Clipboard to move text, tables, and graphic images between Windows-based applications such as from Microsoft Word to Microsoft Excel.

To move information around via the Clipboard, you actually use the Edit menu's Cut, Copy, Paste, and Paste Special commands. So you don't have to know all that much about the Clipboard to make good use of it. One thing you should remember about the Clipboard, however, is that it stores what you've copied or cut temporarily. After you copy or cut, the next time you do so, the previous Clipboard contents are replaced. And when you exit Windows, the Clipboard contents are erased.

Clipboard Viewer; Copying Data; Object Linking and Embedding

Clipboard Viewer The Clipboard Viewer lets you see what's stored on the **Clipboard.** It also lets you save the Clipboard's contents. To start the Clipboard Viewer, display the Main **group** and then double-click the Clipboard Viewer **program item.**

continues

Clipboard *(continued)*

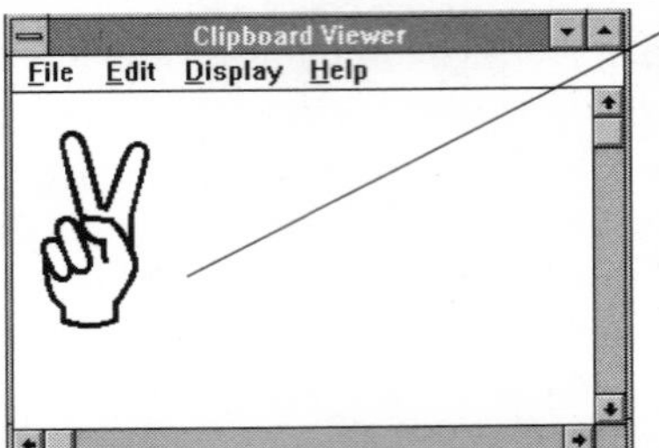

The Clipboard Viewer window shows the Clipboard's current contents. This is a Wingdings character for "Peace, man."

Saving Clipboard Contents

The Clipboard's contents are stored only until the next Copy or Cut operation or until you exit Windows. If you don't want to lose the current Clipboard contents, display the Clipboard Viewer and then follow these steps:

1. Choose the File Save As command.
2. Enter a filename for the Clipboard storage file. You don't enter a file extension. The Clipboard Viewer supplies the correct file extension for you, CLP.
3. Use the Directories and Drives list boxes to specify where the Clipboard file should be located.
4. Choose OK.

Erasing the Clipboard

Choose the Clipboard Viewer's Edit Delete command to erase, or clear, the Clipboard.

Reusing Clipboard Contents

To reuse Clipboard contents you've previously stored in a Clipboard file, display the Clipboard Viewer and then follow these steps:

1. Choose the File Open command.
2. Enter the Clipboard file's filename.
3. If necessary, use the Directories and Drives list boxes to specify where the Clipboard file is located.
4. Choose OK.

Controlling How the Clipboard Viewer Looks

The Clipboard Viewer's Display Menu lists commands that control how the Clipboard contents look. Choose the Display Auto command to show the contents in the same format as when they were placed onto the Clipboard. Or choose one of the other Display menu commands to display the contents in some other format.

Copying Data; Opening Files; Saving Files

Clock

Windows comes with the Clock **accessory.** It tells the time, and it gives the date.

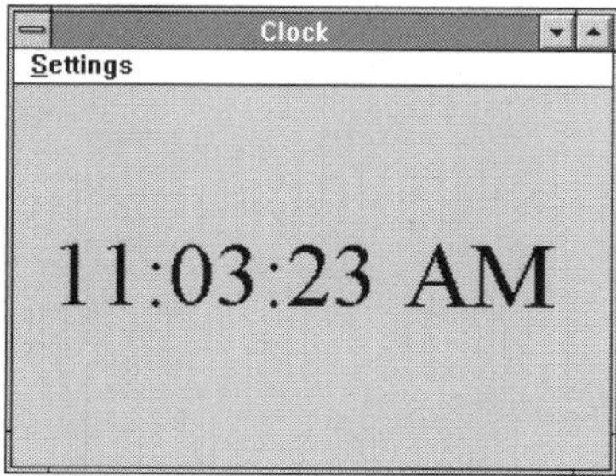

Displaying the Clock

To display the clock, display the Accessories **group** and then double-click the Clock **program item.**

 Program Manager >  Accessories > 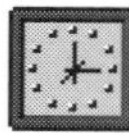 Clock

continues

Clock *(continued)*

Flip-flopping between Digital and Analog Display

The earlier figure of the clock shows a digital display of the time. To switch to an analog display—the same kind a grandfather clock uses—choose the Settings Analog command.

To switch back to the digital display, choose the Settings Digital command.

Displaying Seconds and Date Information

Use the Settings Seconds and Settings Date commands to tell Clock whether you want to see not just the hour and the minute but the seconds and the date. Both commands are switches that turn on and off the display of the seconds or date information.

When the display is turned on, Clock places a check mark in front of the menu command. Apparently, this is in case you don't notice the seconds or date information on the clock face.

Removing the Clock Window's Title Bar

Want to do this? Choose the Settings No Title command. Clock removes both the title bar and the menu bar from its little window.

It's a bit tough to choose commands once the menu bar is gone. So you'll need to remember a trick: To redisplay the menu, press Esc or double-click someplace—it doesn't matter where—on the Clock window.

Changing the Clock Font

You can change the **font** that Clock uses to show date and time information by choosing the Settings Set Font command.

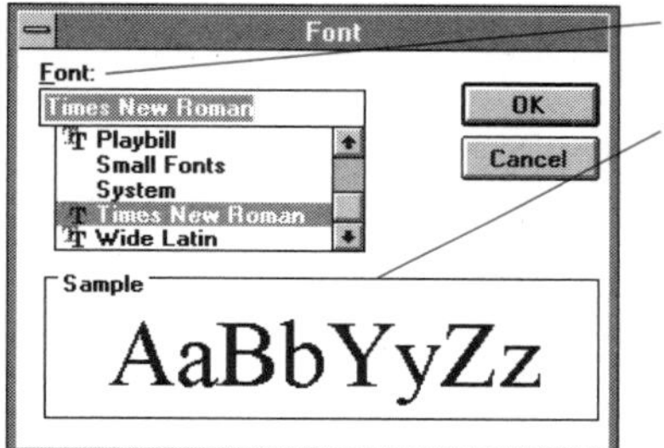

Use the Font list to select the font.

The sample box shows what the selected font looks like.

Closing the Clock

Close, or stop, Clock by closing its application window. You can do this by double-clicking its Control-menu box, by opening its Control menu and choosing Close, or by pressing Alt+F4.

To See the Clock at All Times

Because the clock appears in an application window, it usually only shows when Clock is active, or in the foreground. You can tell Windows it should display the Clock window on top of the active, or foreground, application, however. Just open the Clock's Control menu and choose the Always On Top command.

Closing Applications

Exiting Windows-Based Applications

Closing Documents You close **documents** so that they don't consume **memory**, so that they don't clutter your screen, and so that they don't just plain annoy you.

Closing a Single Document

To close a single document, either double-click its Control-menu box, or be sure the document is visible and then choose its File Close command.

If There Are Unsaved Changes

Most applications won't close a document that you have changed but not yet saved. They will first ask if you want to save your changes. If you say, "Well, yeah, that seems like a good idea," the application then saves the document.

Combo Box Combo box sounds like a special order from a Chinese food take-out place. But it's not. A combo box is a hybrid **dialog box** element that is part **text box** and part **list box**. You can, therefore, enter something into a combo box the way you enter something into a text box. Or you can activate a **drop-down list box** and select an entry from it.

Command Buttons Command buttons tell Windows-based applications that you're ready to do something or that you're not ready to do something. For example, every **dialog box** shows a command button that's labeled OK. If you click the OK button, the Windows-based application knows you're ready to move forward. So clicking OK is your way of giving the Windows-based application the thumbs-up signal.

Most dialog boxes also show the Cancel command button. Cancel means, basically, thumbs down.

Most dialog boxes that deserve the name dialog box also show the **Help** command button. Help means, well, that you need help, of course. When you select Help, the Windows-based application starts the Windows Help program and attempts to turn to the right page of Help information.

Selecting Command Buttons

To choose a command button, you've got three methods. You can click the button with the mouse. You can use the Tab and Shift+Tab keys to highlight the command button with a dark border and then press Enter. (If the button already shows a dark border, you can simply press Enter.) Or, if one of the letters in the command button name is underlined, you can press the Alt key and the underlined letter.

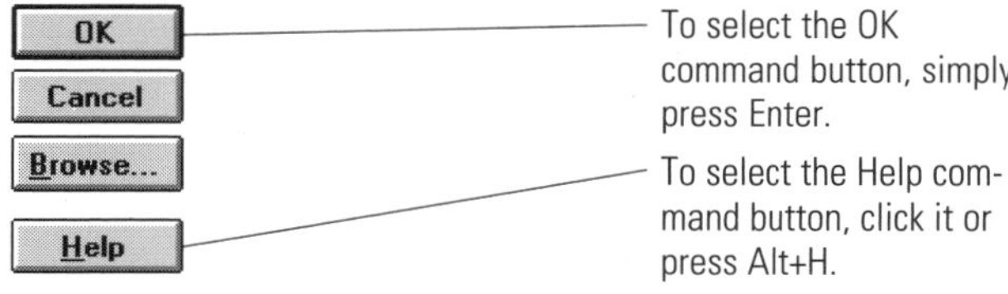

Displaying Additional Options

If the text on a command button is followed by greater than symbols (>>), choosing the button expands the currently displayed dialog box. If the text is followed by ellipses (...), choosing the button displays another dialog box.

Commands

You use commands to tell Windows-based **applications** what you want them to do. For example, you use a command to tell Windows to exit, or close, some application. If an application prints **documents**, you use a command to tell the application you want it to print.

To make your life easier, Windows organizes related commands into sets called **menus**.

Control-menu Commands; Menu Bars; Toolbars

Control-Menu Commands

Control-Menu Commands Control-menu commands appear, not surprisingly, on the Control menus of **application windows, document windows,** and **dialog boxes.**

To open the Control menu of a window or a dialog box, you click the Control-menu box. (It's the little hyphen-in-a-box in the upper left corner of the window or the dialog box.)

Control-menu commands let you manipulate the window or the dialog box in the following ways.

Restore

Undoes the last minimize or maximize command. Handy if you're fooling around with the Control menu and you make a terrible mistake.

Move

Tells Windows you want to move the window or the dialog box. Windows, ever mindful of your feelings, changes the mouse pointer to a four-headed arrow. Once this happens, use the Up and Down direction keys to change the screen position of the window or the dialog box. Press Enter when you're done moving.

Size

Tells Windows you want to change the size of the window. When you choose this command, Windows changes the mouse pointer to a four-headed arrow. You change the window size by using the Up and Down direction keys to move the bottom border and by using the Left and Right direction keys to move the right border. Press Enter when you're done sizing.

Minimize

Tells Windows in no uncertain terms that it should remove the window from the screen. Windows follows your command, but to remind you of the minimized window, it displays a tiny picture, called an **icon**. Because you can't see the Control menu of a minimized window, simply click a minimized window icon to display its Control menu.

Maximize

Tells Windows that it should make the window or the dialog box as big as it can. If you maximize an application window—such as Microsoft Word's—Windows makes the application window as big as your screen. In Word, by the way, document windows can be maximized so that they fill the application window.

Close

Removes the window or the dialog box from the screen. There's more to this command than first meets the eye, however. If you close an application window, you actually close the application. If you close a document window, you also close the document displayed in the document window. If the document hasn't yet been saved, most applications will ask if you want to do this before they close the document. If you close a dialog box, it's the same thing as selecting the Cancel command button.

Next Window

This command—wait a minute. You can guess, right? This command displays the next document window in a stack of document windows.

Switch To

Cool. A power-user tool. This command appears only on the Control menus of application windows. It tells Windows that you want to see Task List—presumably so that you can start another Windows-based application or so that you can move another application you've previously started to the foreground.

Clipboard Viewer; Closing Documents; Control Panel; Switching Tasks

About the Control-menu commands

You won't always see all these commands on a Control menu. Windows displays only those that make sense in the current situation.

Control Panel The Control Panel application lets you change the way Windows operates. To change a Control Panel setting, you start Control Panel. Then you use one of the Settings menu commands or you double-click the appropriate Control Panel Settings **icon**.

Dates and Times; International Settings; Mode; Printers; Virtual Memory; Quick Reference: Control Panel Menu Commands

---

Copying Data You can copy data—such as a value—from one **application** to another or within a Windows-based application by copying the data, which places it on the **Clipboard**, and then pasting the data from the Clipboard to its new location. In general, you do this by selecting the data, choosing the Edit Copy command, positioning the **insertion point** at the place you want to move the data, and then choosing the Edit Paste command.

Moving Data; Sharing Data Among Applications

Copying Files To copy files, you use **File Manager.** To start File Manager, display the Main **group** and double-click the File Manager **program item.**

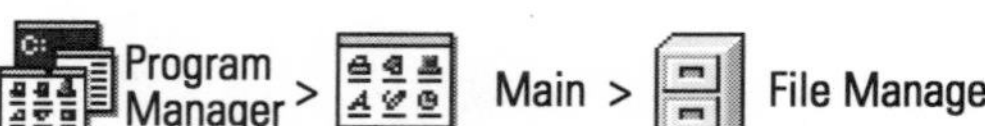

Copying a File to a Floppy with the Mouse

To copy a file to a floppy disk with the mouse, follow these steps:

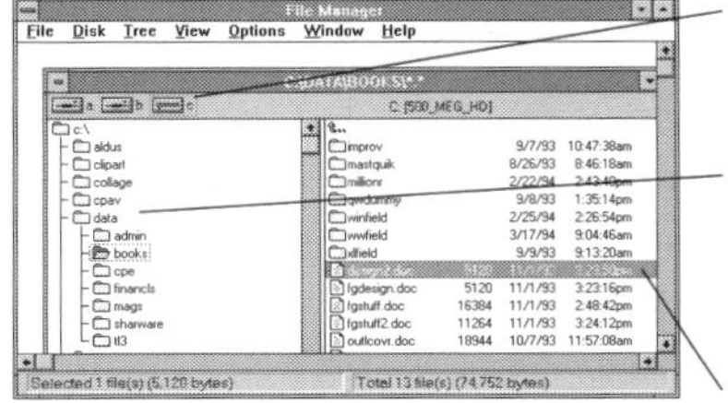

1. Click the icon of the drive that contains the file.
2. Click the directory and, if necessary, double-click the subdirectory that contains the file.
3. Select the file.
4. Drag the file to the floppy disk drive icon.

Copying a File to Another Hard Disk Location with the Mouse

To copy a file to another directory on your hard disk, follow these steps:

1. Click the icon of the drive that contains the file.
2. Click the directory and, if necessary, double-click the subdirectory that contains the file.
3. Select the file.
4. Hold down the Ctrl key.
5. Drag the file to the directory or subdirectory.

continues

Copying Files *(continued)*

Copying a File with the File Copy Command

To copy a file to a floppy disk with the keyboard, follow these steps:

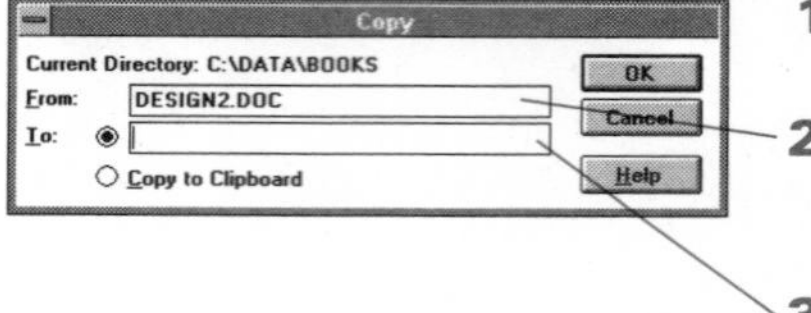

1. Choose the File Copy command.
2. Enter the filename and the path for the file you want to copy.
3. Enter the path for the location to which you want to copy the file—such as A: if you want to copy the file to drive A.
4. Choose OK.

Copying multiple files

To copy multiple files, simply select multiple files. If you're copying files with the mouse, you can select multiple files by clicking on the first file, holding down Shift, and then clicking on the last file. Or you can also hold down Ctrl and then click each file. If you're copying files with the File Copy command, you can use the MS-DOS wildcard characters * and ? in the Copy dialog box's From text box.

Cursor

People sometimes call the **insertion point** a cursor. You can call it that if you want. One of the fun things about being an adult is that you often get to make your own decisions. In this book, I'm going to call the insertion point an insertion point.

Whatever you do, however, don't confuse the terms insertion point and **selection cursor.**

Dates and Times Your computer keeps its own calendar and clock. Windows-based applications will often let you include the date and time from this calendar and clock in their documents. And MS-DOS tags files with the dates and times you create them and modify them. To change your computer's internal, or system, clock, you use **Control Panel.**

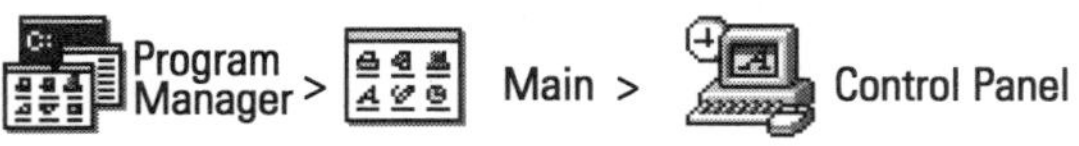

Changing Your System Date and Time

To change your system date or time once you've started Control Panel, follow these steps:

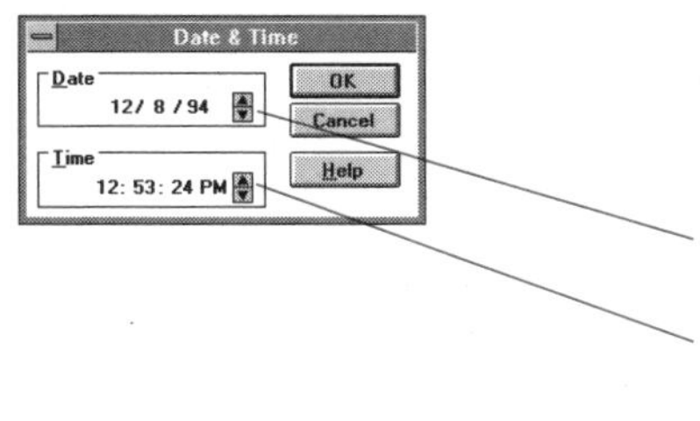

1. Display the Date & Time **dialog box** by double-clicking the Date/Time icon.
2. Use the Date box to change the date.
3. Use the Time box to change the time.

Deleting Files ⁘ **Erasing Files**

Desktop The desktop sounds like something fancy, something you should absolutely know about if you're working with Windows. But really the desktop is nothing all that much. It's the background that appears beneath the Program Manager and application windows.

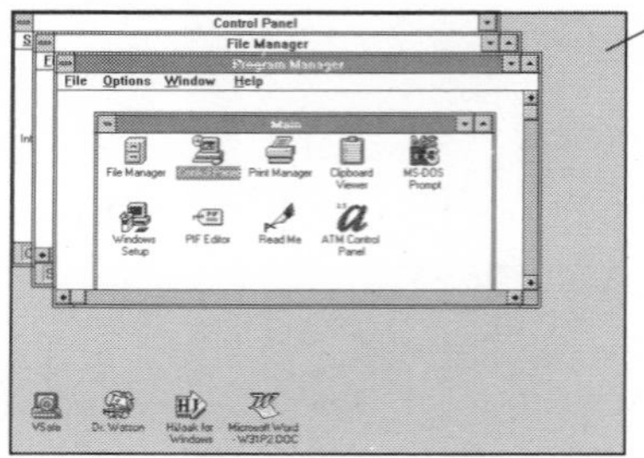

This gray background is the desktop.

Your desktop's appearance depends on the desktop pattern you selected or the **wallpaper** you've said Windows should use to "paper over" the desktop pattern. (This is strange, right? Wallpaper on a desktop? I agree.)

You specify a desktop pattern or wallpaper using the Control Panel's Settings Desktop command.

Switching tasks with a click

If you double-click the desktop—this assumes of course that it's visible—Windows displays Task List. You can move to another application or to Program Manager by double-clicking its name.

Dialog Box A dialog box is simply an on-screen form you fill out to tell Windows or some Windows-based **application** how it should complete some **command**. Any command name followed by ellipses (...) displays a dialog box.

Directory MS-DOS uses directories to organize your disks and the files they store. You can also organize the files in a directory by creating subdirectories. Basically, these directories work like the drawers on a filing cabinet.

You can create directories and see how directories and subdirectories are organized on a disk by using **File Manager**.

Root Directory

Disk Caching Disk caching improves the speed with which your personal computer grabs data from and saves data to your hard disk. We (you and I, that is) don't have time to get into some scholarly discussion of this disk-caching business. But you probably want to know a couple of things.

Caching Read Operations

Disk caching during read operations simply means that your personal computer grabs a bit more data than it really needs, with the idea that the next time your personal computer needs data it may already have it. Basically, caching read operations is akin to grabbing a handful of potato chips from the bowl even though you want to eat only one. When you want to eat that next chip, you won't have to reach for the bowl again.

Caching Write Operations

Disk caching during write operations simply means that your personal computer doesn't save data to your disk every time some eensy teensy bit changes. Instead, it accumulates these changes and then saves them in bigger chunks. Basically, caching write operations is analogous to collecting garbage in a can under the sink and then emptying this garbage out whenever the can gets full. (In no way, of course, do I mean to imply that your data is garbage. It's just the best metaphor I can think of.)

SmartDrive

Directory Window A directory window is the **document window** that **File Manager** displays to show you how the active disk's directories are organized and which files are in the active directory.

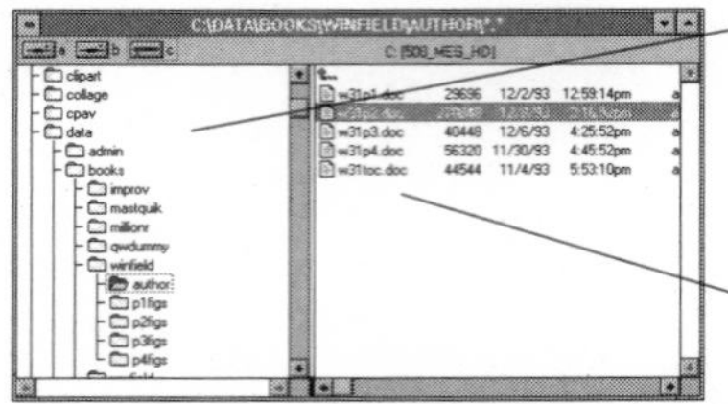

On the left half of the directory window, File Manager shows the directory organization in a tree.

On the right half of the directory window, File Manager shows the subdirectory and files in the active directory.

Documents A document is what gets displayed in the **document window** that an **application** displays. In the case of a word processor, this name works pretty nicely. The report, letter, or memo that a word processor displays in a document window inside its application is, well, basically a document. Right?

Unfortunately, the "document" label doesn't work as well when it's used to name other applications' displayed information. The spreadsheet that a spreadsheet program such as Lotus 1-2-3 or Microsoft Excel displays is also, technically speaking, a document; it gets displayed in a document window. The checkbook register an accounting program such as Quicken or Microsoft Money displays is, I guess, a document since it gets displayed in a document window.

Document Window The document window is the rectangle that an **application** uses to display your **documents.** If you have more than one document open, the **application window** stacks the documents, one on top of the other. You may not be able to see any but the active document window, however, unless you tile the open document windows or resize the top document window so that it doesn't fill the application window.

Control-Menu Commands

Double-Click To double-click some object simply means that you **click** it twice in a row. Quickly. Click-click.

Now that you know what double-click means, let me give you some example double-click operations. You can double-click group **icons** and minimized window icons to open their windows. You can double-click **program items** to start the programs that the items represent. You can also double-click an application's Control-menu box to close the **application window** and exit the application.

DoubleSpace MS-DOS version 6 and later comes with a disk compression utility, DoubleSpace. It lets you scrunch, or compress, files so that they take less disk space.

If Windows version 3.1 and MS-DOS version 6 or later came with your personal computer, you may be able to see information about disks you've compressed with the DoubleSpace utility by starting **File Manager** and choosing its Tools DoubleSpace Info command.

 Program Manager >  Main >  File Manager

Drag

Drag is a shortcut description for this three-step sequence:

1 You move the mouse pointer so that it rests over some object—such as a **program item**.
2 You press and hold down the mouse's left button.
3 You move the mouse pointer. As you move the mouse pointer, Windows moves, or drags, the object.

People in the know refer to the entire process as dragging the object. If you move a program item with the mouse, for example, you say that you dragged the item.

Click; Double-Click; Drag-and-Drop

Drag-and-Drop

Drag-and-drop is a technique that lets you move and copy pieces of a **document** with the mouse. Drag-and-drop works in many spreadsheet and word processor applications.

Moving with Drag-and-Drop

To move some piece of a document—such as a line of text, a paragraph, or a picture—select it and then drag it to its new location.

Copying with Drag-and-Drop

To copy some piece of a document—such as a chunk of text or a picture—select it, press Ctrl, and then drag it to its new location.

Click; Drag; Object Linking and Embedding

Copying data between applications

You can often use drag-and-drop techniques to copy data between application windows. Microsoft Word and Excel, for example, let you drag-and-drop from their application windows. When you do, you create linked objects.

Drop-Down List Boxes A drop-down list box is a **list box** that doesn't show its list until you tell it to. To tell a drop-down list box it should display its list, click the down arrow at the end of the box, or select the list box and press Alt+Down.

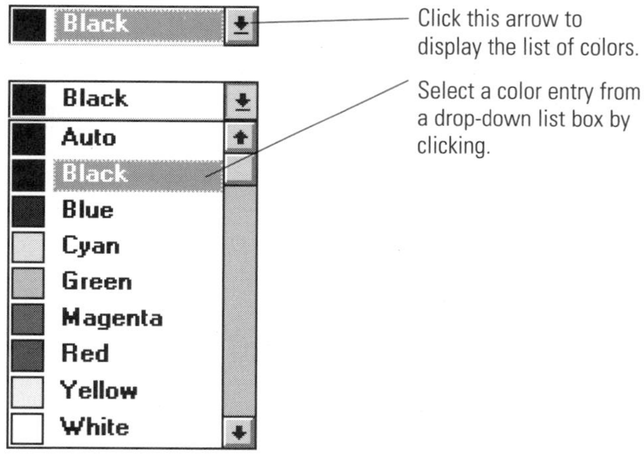

Click this arrow to display the list of colors.

Select a color entry from a drop-down list box by clicking.

Drop-and-Drag I think this is the name of a TV show about hunting. It's on one of the cable stations. I mention this only so you don't confuse the TV show with the similarly named feature available in many Windows-based applications, **Drag-and-Drop.**

Dr. Watson Dr. Watson, as you probably know, was Sherlock Holmes's sidekick. In Sir Arthur Conan Doyle's short stories and novel, Dr. Watson documented Holmes's progress in a case.

Windows comes with a Dr. Watson utility that works in a fashion similar to Doyle's fictional physician. When Windows encounters an **application error**, Dr. Watson detects this, records a bunch of system information, and displays a **dialog box** that lets you describe any suspicious events leading up to the error.

Starting the Dr. Watson Utility

To use the Dr. Watson utility every time you use Windows, set up a DRWATSON.EXE **program item** in the StartUp **group** by following these steps:

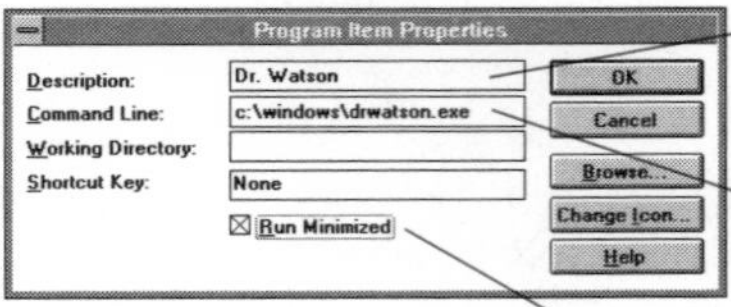

1. Display the StartUp group window.
2. Choose the File New command.
3. Mark the Program Item option button and press Enter.
4. Enter Dr. Watson in the Description text box.
5. Enter *c:\windows\drwatson.exe* in the Command Line text box.
6. Mark the Run Minimized check box.
7. Press Enter.

Using the Dr. Watson Utility

Dr. Watson collects all its evidence—I mean information—in a **Notepad** file named DRWATSON.LOG. If you contact a software developer's technical support department about an error you've encountered, the support person may find the information in the DRWATSON.LOG file helpful. You open the DRWATSON.LOG file using the Notepad application.

Entering Text To enter text into a **document**, you simply use the keyboard to type the characters. Tap, tap, tap. No joke. That's all there is to it.

Erasing You can erase the preceding **character** by pressing Backspace.

You can erase the current selection—a character, a word, or the contents of some **text box**—by pressing the Del key or the Backspace key. Some **applications** also provide an Edit Clear **command**.

Erasing Files **Documents** and other important files such as application files get stored on disk. To erase a file in the Windows operating environment—such as a document file—you use **File Manager**.

Erasing Files with File Manager

To erase a file once you've started File Manager, follow these steps:

1. Click the disk drive icon of the drive that contains the file.
2. Click the directory and if necessary double-click the subdirectory that contains the file or files you want to erase.
3. Select the file or files you want to erase.
4. Choose the File Delete command.
5. When File Manager asks, confirm that you do want to delete the file.

Unerasing Files

Exiting Windows To exit Windows, choose Program Manager's File Exit command or close the Program Manager window. Windows closes, or exits from, any open Windows-based applications and then closes Windows.

Exiting Windows-Based Applications; Window Buttons

Exiting Windows-Based Applications To exit just about any Windows-based application, you can choose the File Exit command. Or you can close the **application window** by double-clicking its Control-menu box. In general, an application will ask if you want to save documents that have unsaved changes.

Closing Documents; Saving Files; Window Buttons

File **Applications** and **documents** get stored on disk as files. For example, the document file you create with **Write** gets stored on disk as a file. And the **File Manager** program gets stored on disk as a file.

File Manager File Manager lets you copy, move, and delete files. It also lets you format and label floppy disks. To start File Manager, display the Main group and double-click File Manager.

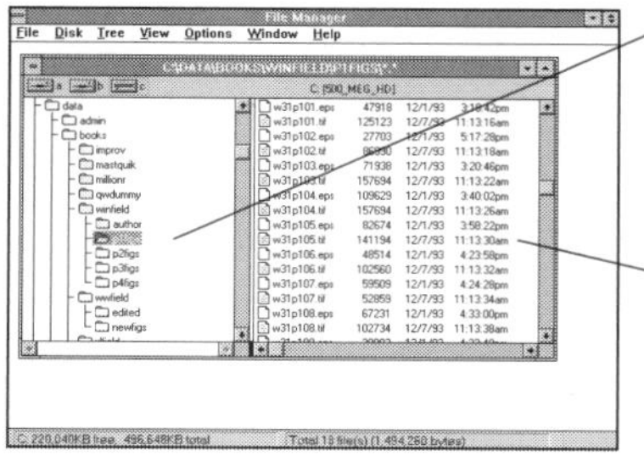

File Manager uses a **directory window** to show the directory structure and the files in the active directory.

File Manager provides file information such as the file size in kilobytes and the last modification date. Refer to your MS-DOS user documentation or a big book about MS-DOS if you have questions about any of these pieces of information.

Selecting Disks

To select a disk, click on the disk drive **icon.**

Selecting Directories

To select a directory, scroll through the tree pane in the directory window until you see the directory. Then click the directory.

If the directory is a subdirectory in another directory, you may need to first select the parent directory and display its subdirectories. You can do this by double-clicking the parent directory. Or you can also choose the Tree Expand All command to display all the subdirectories in the tree.

File Manager alerts you to subdirectories

If you choose the Tree Indicate Expandable Branches command, File Manager adds the plus sign (+) to the directory icons representing directories that have subdirectories.

continues

File Manager *(continued)*

Selecting Files

To select a file in the active directory, scroll through the directory pane in the directory window until you see the file. Then click the file.

You can select multiple files by clicking on the first file, holding down Shift, and then clicking on the last file. Or you can also hold down Ctrl and then click each file.

Understanding File Manager's Disk and File Icons

File Manager uses different types of icons to represent directories and the various types of files. If you've come this far, you'll probably find it helpful to know what the different icons represent. Here is a list of the File Manager icons:

Icon	Description
	Represents a directory. If the directory is open, the folder appears open. If the directory is inactive, the folder is closed. If the directory holds subdirectories and you've chosen the Tree Indicate Expandable Branches command, File Manager adds a plus sign (+) to the front of the folder.
	Represents an application file. You can start the application by double-clicking it or by selecting it and choosing the File Run command.
	Represents an associated document file. You can start the associated application and open this file by double-clicking it or by selecting it and choosing the File Run command.
	Represents an unassociated document file. You can't open this file from File Manager.

Associating Files; Copying Files; Erasing Files; Formatting Floppies; Moving Files; Renaming Files; Troubleshooting: Finding Lost Files; Unerasing Files

Filenames You usually give a **document** its filename when you choose the application's File Save As command.

File-Naming Rules

MS-DOS file-naming rules apply to Windows-based application document files. A filename can't have more than eight characters. All numbers and letters that appear on your keyboard are OK. And so are many other characters. You can't, however, use characters that MS-DOS expects to be used in special ways on its command line such as spaces, asterisks, and question marks. If you need more information than this, refer to the MS-DOS user documentation that almost surely came with your computer.

Specifying File Extensions

The MS-DOS file extension, by the way, isn't something you need to worry about. Windows-based applications usually supply the file extension to identify file type. Microsoft Word, for example, uses the file extension DOC. Microsoft Excel uses the file extension XLS.

Fonts Windows lets you use a variety of fonts in your documents. With fonts, you can even add Greek symbols and other special characters to your document. Here are just a few examples of **TrueType** fonts:

Arial resembles Helvetica.

Braggadocio is, well, rather bold.

Courier New looks like typewriter output.

DESDEMONA IS REALLY RATHER FUNKY, DON'T YOU AGREE?

continues

Fonts *(continued)*

Times New Roman uses serifs—little cross-strokes—to make characters easier to read.

ΑΣΔΦαβχψυσΩΙΥ — These are TrueType Symbol characters.

☒❖⌘●&ер☠✡✞ — These are TrueType Wingdings characters.

Foreground Applications

Windows lets you run more than one **application** at a time. The foreground application is the application that your commands affect and the application with the window that appears in front of the other application windows on your screen.

You can change which application runs in the foreground by clicking a background application's window or by using the Control menu's Switch To command.

People sometimes refer to foreground applications as "active applications" because they appear in what Windows terms "active windows." This isn't a very good description, however. It's quite likely that the foreground application isn't the only one that's active. **Background applications** that you or Windows started are also active. (It may be, by the way, that these applications are "less active" because they often get fewer system resources.)

Switching Tasks

Formatting Floppies

Use **File Manager** to format floppy disks.

Formatting a Floppy Disk

To format a floppy disk once you've started File Manager and inserted the floppy disk into its drive, follow these steps:

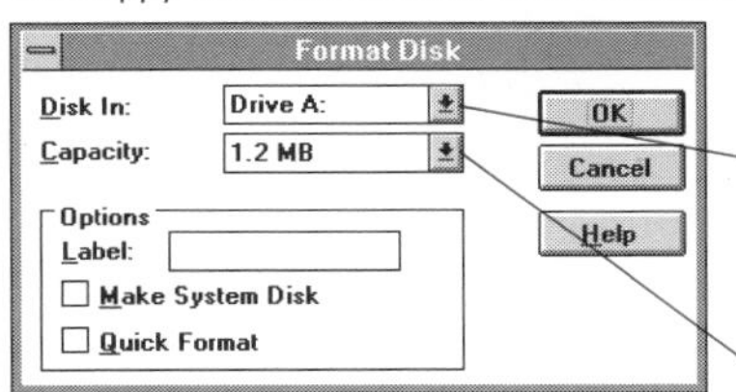

1. Choose the Disk Format Disk command.
2. Activate the Disk In drop-down list box and select the floppy disk drive.
3. Activate the Capacity drop-down list box and select the floppy disk density.
4. Choose OK.
5. Select Yes when File Manager asks you to confirm that it should format the disk.
6. Select No when File Manager finishes and asks if you want to format another disk—unless, of course, you do want to format another disk.

Games

Windows version 3.1 comes with a couple of games: Solitaire and Minesweeper. You can get lots of other Windows games too. Below is an example Solitaire hand.

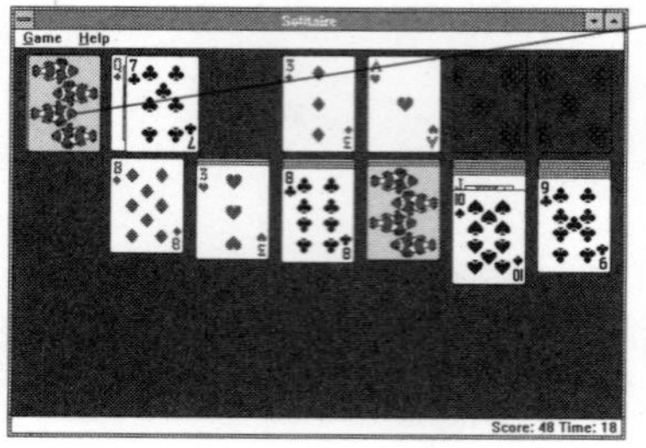

Click the deck to see your next card.

Drag cards to move them to another stack.

I'm not going to describe how you play these games. Mostly, you just click and drag. I will say, however, that the games are a pretty good way to get comfortable with your mouse.

This last little nugget of knowledge also suggests a useful explanation in case your boss wonders why you're fooling around. "Oh, geez, Boss, I didn't know you were standing behind me. . . . Well, no, I'm not playing games. No way. I just read in that Field Guide that you can hone your mouse skills this way."

Groups

Program Manager organizes your applications into sets—in a manner akin to the way your mother may have organized your clothes in a dresser when you were younger. Socks. Underwear. Shirts. You get the picture, right?

Each of those little pictures, or **icons,** you see in Program Manager is a group. To see a list of the groups, you can open Program Manager's Window menu. It will list numbered commands for each of the groups.

Peeking in a Group Window

You can do your own organizing by creating groups and adding program items to them. To display a group window, double-click the group icon or choose the Windows menu command that names the group.

Creating a Group

To create a group, follow these steps:

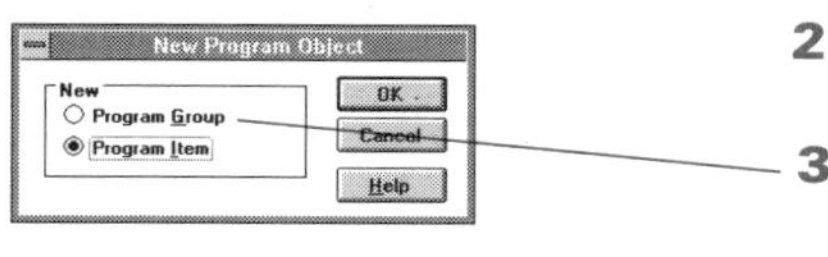

1. Display Program Manager.
2. Choose the File New command.
3. Mark the Program Group option button and press Enter.
4. Enter a name for the group in the Description text box.
5. Press Enter. (You don't have to fill in the Group File text box.)

Deleting a Group

To delete a group, follow these steps:

1. Display Program Manager.
2. Select the Group.
3. Choose the File Delete command.

Renaming a Group

To rename a group, follow these steps:

1. Display Program Manager.
2. Select the Group.
3. Choose the File Properties command.
4. When Program Manager displays the Program Group Properties dialog box, edit the contents of the Description text box.

Program Items; StartUp Group

Help

Windows itself and almost all Windows-based applications and accessories include an online help feature that means information is almost always just a click or a keystroke away. You access this help by using one of the Help menu commands. The Help menu usually appears as the rightmost menu on an application's **menu bar.**

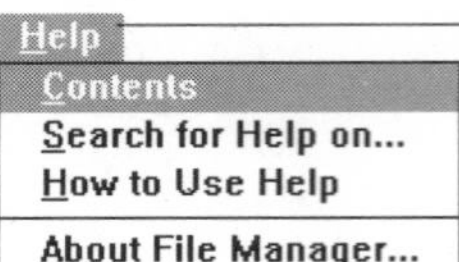

Help menus vary, but most closely resemble the File Manager Help menu shown here.

Using the Help Contents Command

Choose the Help Contents command to display a list of the major categories of Help topics. When you do, Windows starts the Help application and displays the list.

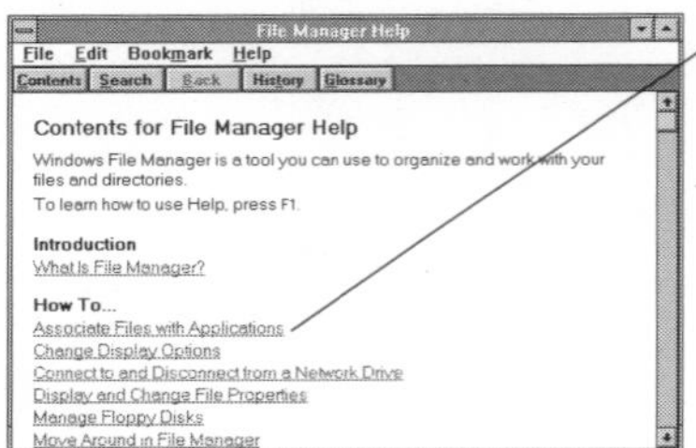

To see a list of the topics within a category, click the category. To see information on one of the topics that Help next lists, click that topic.

Getting back to the contents list

Select the Contents command button to return to the list of major categories of Help topics—the same list you see when you choose the Help Contents command.

Using the Help Search Command

Choose the Help Search for Help On command or select the Help application window's Search command button to display an alphabetic list of the Help topics and subtopics. When you do, Windows starts the Help application and displays its Search dialog box.

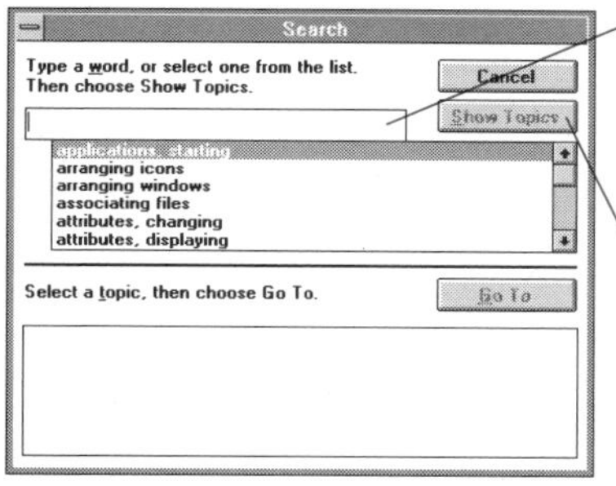

1 Enter the topic category name or scroll through the top list box to find the topic category.

2 Select the Show Topics command button.

3 Select the topic from the bottom list box.

Using the How to Use Help Command

When you start Help from a particular application, what really happens is that Windows starts another application named Help and tells this other application to open a heavily indexed file of information about the particular application.

If you choose the Help How to Use Help command, this same basic sequence occurs with one exception. Windows doesn't tell Help to open a file of information about the particular application. Instead, Windows tells Help to open a file of information about the Help application.

Help on other applications

Once you've started the Help application, you can use its File Open command to open any of the Help files stored on your hard disk. Help files use the application file name and the file extension HLP. Help files usually reside in the application's directory. (The Windows Help application files reside in the Windows directory.)

continues

Help *(continued)*

About the Help About Command

The Help About command doesn't really give help.

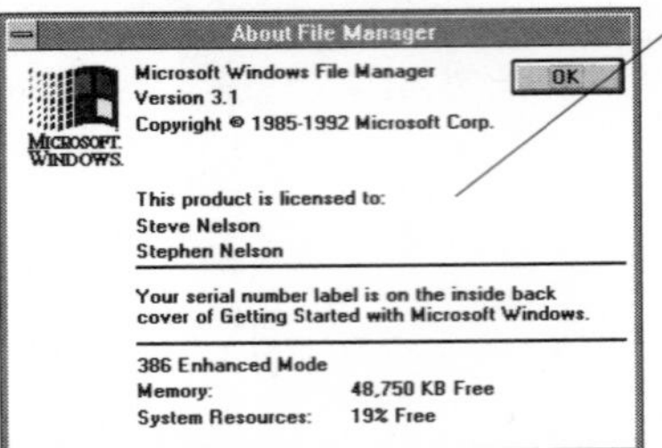

The Help About command displays information about the application and, in some cases, about the system resources.

Help Glossary

Help Glossary If you see a colored term with a dotted underline in the Help application window, it means there's a glossary entry, or definition, for the term.

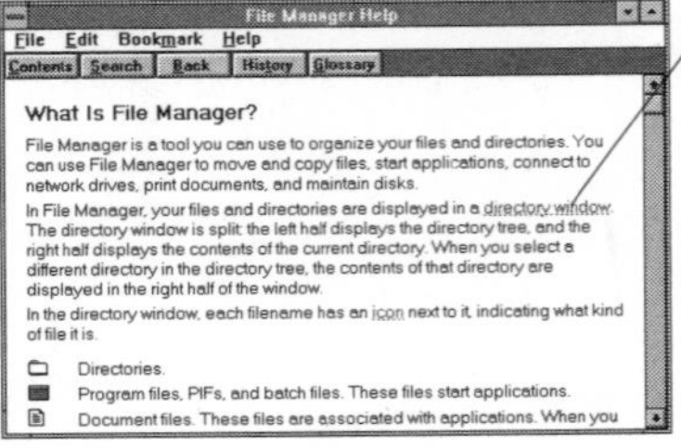

To see the definition, click the term.

directory window
A File Manager window that displays the contents of a disk. The window shows both the directory tree and the contents of the current directory. A directory window is a document window that you can move, size, reduce, or enlarge.

Help displays glossary information in a **pop-up box**. Press any key or click anywhere to close the pop-up box.

Icons

An icon is simply a visual image, or picture, that represents something else. In Windows and Windows-based **applications**, icons represent things such as **groups**, **program items**, and **minimized windows.**

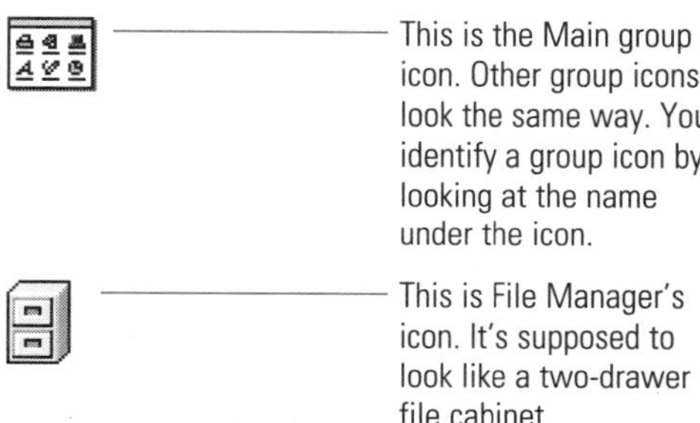

This is the Main group icon. Other group icons look the same way. You identify a group icon by looking at the name under the icon.

This is File Manager's icon. It's supposed to look like a two-drawer file cabinet.

Insertion Point

The insertion point is the vertical bar that shows where what you type gets placed. If this seems unclear to you, start a Windows-based application such as **Write**, begin typing, and look at the bar that moves ahead of the text you type. See it? That's the insertion point.

International Settings

You can customize Windows so that it uses the appropriate language and currency symbol and formats dates and times so they look right. To do these things, start **Control Panel** and choose the Settings International command.

continues

International Settings *(continued)*

You don't have to use the Settings menu commands. You can double-click the icons in the Control Panel window.

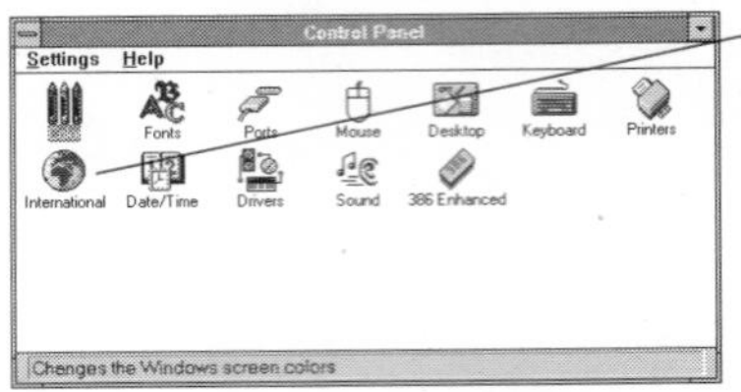

Double-clicking the International icon is equivalent to choosing the Settings International command.

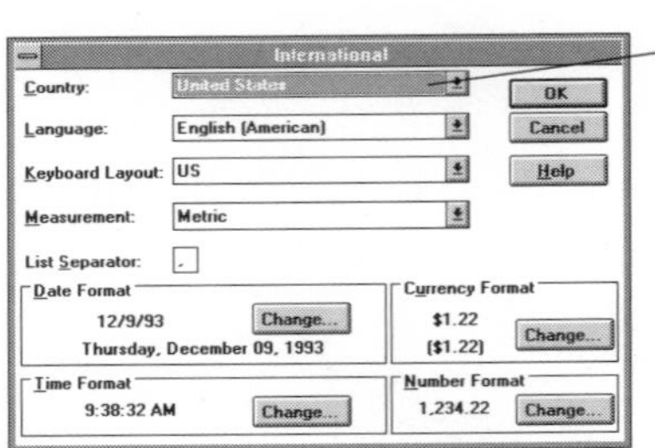

When you choose the Settings International command, Control Panel displays the International dialog box.

Changing the Country

Choose an entry from the Country **list box** to change the Date, Time, Currency, and Number formats all in one fell swoop.

Changing the Language

Choose an entry from the Language list box to change the language. Windows-based applications take their cue from the language selection to do things like check spelling, alphabetize, and so on.

Changing the Keyboard Layout

You can guess how this works, right? You activate the Keyboard Layout list box and choose the entry that describes your keyboard.

Specifying English or Metric Measurement

Use the Measurement drop-down list box entries—English and Metric—to specify which units of measurement you want Windows-based applications to use.

Changing the List Separator

Use the List Separator text box to specify which character Windows should use to separate the items in a list.

Changing the Date and Time Format

To change the way Windows-based applications display dates and times, choose the Change button in the Date Format or Time Format boxes. Control Panel displays a dialog box that provides a bunch of boxes and buttons you use to describe exactly how you want the date or time to appear. After you make your selections, choose OK.

Changing the Currency Format

To change the way Windows-based applications display currency amounts, choose the Change button in the Currency Format box. Control Panel displays a dialog box that asks where the symbol should appear (before or after the value), how negative values should appear, and which currency you want to use. After you make your selections, choose OK.

Entering currency symbols

You can enter a currency symbol that doesn't show on the keyboard as an **ANSI character** (assuming that the character is an ANSI character, of course). Or you can use the **Character Map** accessory.

continues

International Settings *(continued)*

Changing the Number Format

To change the way Windows-based applications display numbers—well, you can guess how this goes by now—choose the Change button in the Number Format box. Then, when Control Panel displays the Number dialog box, indicate how Windows-based applications should separate thousands (such as with a comma), how they should separate decimal places (such as with a period), how many decimal places should be displayed (such as two decimal places), and whether leading zeros should be displayed. When you're done, choose OK.

Keyboard Shortcuts

Keyboard shortcuts are key combinations you can use to select a menu command. So, rather than having to open a **menu** and then select a **command** from the menu and then press Enter, you press two or three keys. Often the Alt or Ctrl key is one of those used.

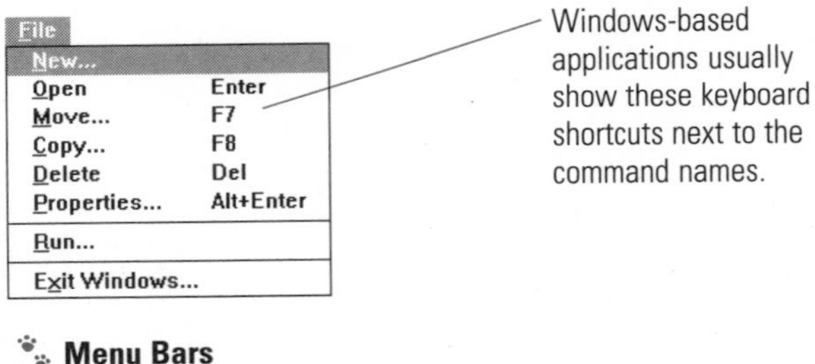

Windows-based applications usually show these keyboard shortcuts next to the command names.

Menu Bars

List Boxes

If there are only a limited set of choices that make sense in a given situation and a Windows-based application knows those choices, it will display a list. Your life is then easier—all you have to do is select one or more of the list's entries.

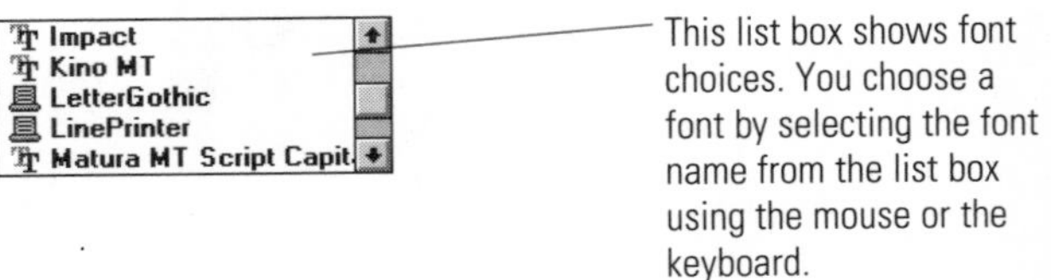

This list box shows font choices. You choose a font by selecting the font name from the list box using the mouse or the keyboard.

Selecting a Single List Entry

You can select a single list entry by clicking it and pressing Enter. Or you can select a single list entry by highlighting it with the direction keys and pressing Enter.

Selecting Multiple List Entries

If you want to select more than one list entry—and the application will let you—you can do that too. (This wouldn't make sense in the case of a font choice, but it might if you were selecting files to open from a list.) You can select a contiguous range of list entries by clicking the first list entry and then dragging the mouse to the last list entry. You can also highlight the first list entry, hold down the Shift key, and then press the Down direction key to select additional list entries.

If you want to select a noncontiguous set of list entries, hold down the Ctrl key and then click the entries you want to select.

Activating a Drop-Down List Box

If a Windows-based application doesn't have room to display the list box—and this is the usual case—it will use a drop-down list box. In this case, you don't see the list until you activate, or drop down, the list by clicking the arrow.

Combo Boxes

Reviewing your choices

You can usually move to a list entry by typing the first character of a list entry. If you're at the start of a list viewing the entries that begin with the letter "A" but want to move to the last part of the list that shows the entries that begin with the letter "Z," type *Z*.

Macro **Recorder**

Media Player You use the Media Player application to play multimedia files, such as sound or animation, and to control multimedia devices such as compact disc or videodisc players.

Memory Memory is the temporary storage area your computer uses while it's running MS-DOS, Windows, and applications. What is stored in memory is lost when you turn off your computer. So that's kind of a bummer. But you can usually save stuff you want to store permanently by saving it to disk.

Saving Files; Virtual Memory

Menu Bars The menu bar is the row of menu names that usually appears beneath the application title bar. You will notice a similarity when you compare Windows-based applications from the same software developer. Microsoft's Windows-based applications tend to use the same menus. Lotus Development's Windows-based applications tend to use the same menus.

File Edit View Insert Format Tools Table Window Help

The menu bars in Microsoft's Windows-based applications—such as those that come with Microsoft Office—often look the same.

Commands; Toolbars

Menus Menus list **commands.** Ideally, a menu is supposed to segregate commands into sets of related commands.

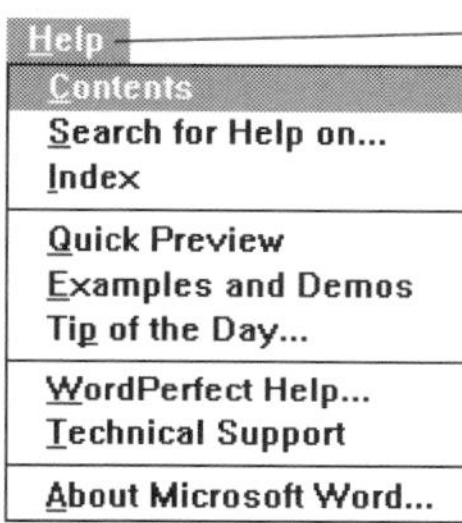

This is the Microsoft Word Help menu. Activate it by clicking or by pressing Alt and the underlined letter in the menu name, H.

 **Menu Bars; Toolbars**

Message Box A message box is simply a miniature **dialog box** with a message from a Windows-based application. It usually has some **command buttons**, such as OK and Cancel.

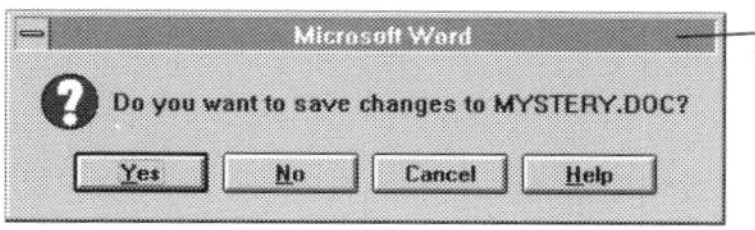

This is the message box Microsoft Word displays if you try to close a document with unsaved changes. Rather than OK and Cancel, it uses Yes and No command buttons.

Minimized Windows A minimized window is one you've told Windows to shrink so that it shows as an **icon**, or a tiny picture.

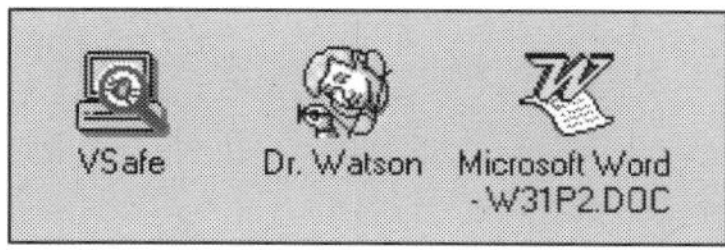

Minimized windows appear as icons, or tiny pictures. These are minimized application windows. They appear on the Windows **desktop**.

continues

Minimized Windows *(continued)*

Minimizing Windows

You can minimize application windows and document windows by choosing the Minimize command from the window's Control menu or by clicking the down arrow button in the upper right corner of the window. A minimized application window appears on the Windows desktop. A minimized **document window** appears in its **application window.**

Unminimizing Windows

To unminimize a shrunken window, double-click the icon.

 **Control-Menu Commands; Window Buttons**

Mode

You can run Windows version 3.1 in two modes: standard and 386 enhanced. Standard mode is essentially a crippled version of Windows that doesn't do a lot of really cool things that the 386 enhanced mode does. The 386 enhanced mode, for example, uses **virtual memory,** which means, among other things, that you can really do **multitasking.**

People sometimes have to use the standard mode, however, because their computers aren't powerful enough to run 386 enhanced mode. If you're running a personal computer that uses the Intel 80286 processor or that doesn't have much memory, you'll need to use the standard mode. If you're running a personal computer that uses an Intel 80386 processor or higher and that possesses at least 2 megabytes of memory, you'll want to use 386 enhanced mode.

In fact, if your computer has an 80386 processor or higher and has more than 2 megabytes of memory, Windows runs in the 386 enhanced mode. Otherwise, Windows runs in standard mode. If you want to force Windows to run in standard mode, start Windows by typing *win /s* at the MS-DOS prompt. The /s tells Windows to run in standard mode.

Curious about which mode Windows is running?

You can learn which mode Windows is running in by displaying the Program Manager and choosing the Help About command.

Moving Data You can move data—such as a chunk of text—from one application to another or within a Windows-based application by cutting the data and placing it on the **Clipboard** and then pasting the data from the Clipboard to its new location. In general, you do this by selecting the data, choosing the Edit Cut command (or pressing Shift+Del), positioning the **insertion point** at the place you want to move the data, and then choosing the Edit Paste command (or pressing Shift+Ins).

Copying Data; Sharing Data Among Applications

Moving Files To move files, you use **File Manager**. To start File Manager, display the Main **group** and double-click the File Manager **program item**.

 Program Manager >  Main >  File Manager

continues

Moving Files *(continued)*

Moving a File to Another Hard Disk Location with the Mouse

To move a file to another directory on your hard disk, follow these steps:

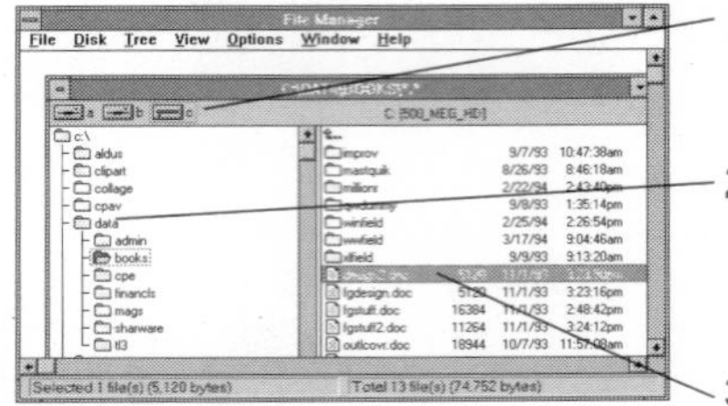

1 Click the icon of the disk drive that contains the file.

2 Click the directory and, if necessary, double-click the subdirectory that contains the file.

3 Select the file.

4 Drag the file to the directory or subdirectory.

Moving a File with the Keyboard

To move a file with the keyboard, follow these steps:

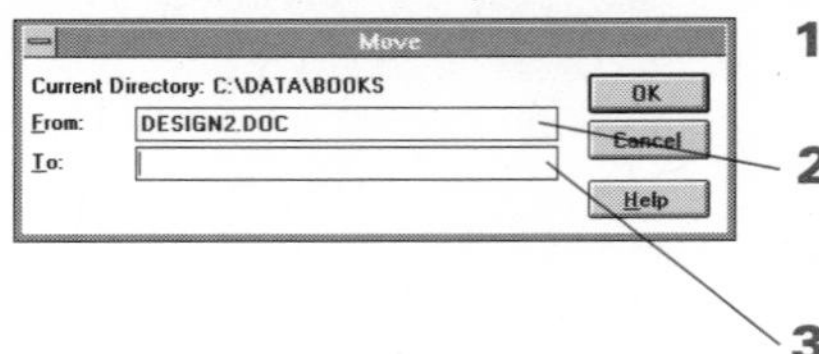

1 Choose the File Move command.

2 Enter the path and the filename for the file you want to move.

3 Enter the path for the location to which you want to move the file—such as A: if you want to move the file to drive A.

4 Choose OK.

Copying Files

MS-DOS Prompt The MS-DOS Prompt **program item**, which usually appears in the Main **group,** displays the MS-DOS command prompt so that you can do whatever you do with the MS-DOS prompt—such as type MS-DOS commands.

 Program Manager >  Main >  MS-DOS Prompt

By the way, in case you're interested, what the MS-DOS program item really does is start a second copy of the COMMAND.COM command. It doesn't return you to your original command prompt. COMMAND.COM displays the MS-DOS prompt and tries to figure out the stuff you type after the prompt. You probably didn't actually care about this, though, did you? I should have known better. Sorry.

Multitasking Multitasking refers to the running of more than one **application**. You may not care about this, but Windows lets you multitask. You can be working away with your word processor, for example, at the same time that **Print Manager** is slaving away printing your budget spreadsheet. Windows automatically multitasks Windows-based applications. Whenever you or Windows open, or start, more than one Windows-based application, you're multitasking. (Pretty cool, huh?)

To switch between the applications you're running, you use the Control menu's Switch To command.

 **PIF; PIF Editor; Switching Tasks**

Multitasking MS-DOS applications

If you want to multitask MS-DOS applications, you'll need to adjust the MS-DOS application's PIF—something you do using the PIF Editor application.

Notepad

The Notepad **accessory** is a simple word processor. You can use it to jot down quick notes. You can use it to view and edit your CONFIG.SYS and AUTOEXEC.BAT. (Don't worry. If you don't know what these things are, you don't want to view or edit them.)

Starting Notepad

To start Notepad, display the Accessories group and then double-click the Notepad program item.

 Program Manager >  Accessories >  Notepad

Creating a Note

To create a note, simply begin typing with the keyboard.

If you want Notepad to **word wrap** your lines of text, choose the Edit Word Wrap command.

To edit text you've already entered, first select the character or block of text you want to change. (You can do this by clicking just before the first character you want to change and then dragging the mouse to just after the last character you want to change.) Next type the new text you want to replace the old text.

You can erase the preceding character by pressing Backspace.

You can erase the current selection—a character, a sentence, a picture, or a paragraph—by pressing the Del key.

Finding Text

Choose the Search Find command to find text within a **document**.

Choose the Search Find Next command to repeat the last search you specified with the Search Find command.

Printing a Note

Choose the File Print command to print the note.

Saving a Note

To save your note to disk, follow these steps:

1. Choose the File Save As command.
2. Enter a filename for the document. You don't enter a file extension. Notepad supplies the correct file extension for you, TXT.
3. Use the Directories and Drives list boxes to specify where the note file should be located.
4. Choose OK.

Retrieving a Note

To retrieve a note you've previously stored on disk, start Notepad and then follow these steps:

1. Choose the File Open command.
2. Enter the file name of the note.
3. If necessary, use the Directories and Drives list boxes to specify where the note is located.
4. Choose OK.

Opening Files; Saving Files; Write

Date- and time-stamping notes

If you use LOG (instead of TXT) as the file extension for a note and type *.LOG* at the left margin of the top line of the note, Notepad automatically adds lines of text to the end of the note that describe the last modification date and time for the Notepad file. You can also place the current system date and time in a note by choosing the Edit Time/Date command.

Object

The word **object** gets my vote as the most over-used and therefore least useful technoterm. The word is used in at least a dozen ways. In drawing programs, the term often refers to the lines and shapes you draw. In some database programs, the term refers to the building blocks that constitute your database. In programming, the term can refer to items your program manipulates. And, oh yes. One of the other ways the term is used is to refer to OLE objects, which are chunks of documents you copy or move between **applications.**

Object Linking and Embedding

Object Linking and Embedding

Object linking and embedding, or OLE, is a Windows feature.

What OLE Does

You use OLE to create what's called a compound document—a document file that combines two or more types of documents. For example, you might want to create a compound document that includes a long report written in, for example, Microsoft Word. On page 27 of your report, however, you might want to include a worksheet (or a worksheet fragment) created in Lotus 1-2-3. And perhaps on page 37 of your report, you might want to include a chart created in Microsoft Excel. So your compound document really consists of stuff created in different applications and pasted together into one big, compound document.

Using OLE to Create Compound Documents

To do all this pasting together and combining, you can often use the application's Edit Copy and Edit Paste (or Edit Paste Special) commands. Microsoft applications such as Excel and Word also include Insert Object commands that let you add and create objects for a compound document. You indicate whether you want an object linked or embedded when you use the Edit Paste, Edit Paste Special, or Insert Object command.

Distinguishing Between Linked Objects and Embedded Objects

A linked object—remember this might be the Excel worksheet you've pasted into a word-processing document—gets updated whenever the source document changes. An embedded object doesn't. (You can, however, double-click an embedded object to open the application that created the embedded object to make your changes.)

Drag-and-Drop

What you absolutely need to know about OLE

Perhaps the most important tidbit for you to know about OLE is that it's very easy to use. You don't have to do anything other than copy and paste the things—called objects—you want to plop into the compound document. If you're working with applications that support the newest version of OLE, you may also be able to drag-and-drop things between application windows.

Object Packager

The Object Packager **accessory** makes it easier for you to embed and link objects. In a nutshell, what Object Packager lets you do is create an **icon** for an object, insert the icon into a compound document, and then describe the object that the icon represents.

 Program Manager >  Main >  Object Packager

Clipboard; Object Linking and Embedding

Opening Files

Opening Files You can open both **application** files and **document** files. You do this using either **Program Manager** or **File Manager**.

Opening Application Files

You open application files when you start the application—for example, by double-clicking the application's **program item** or by double-clicking an application file listed in the File Manager **directory window**.

Opening Document Files

You open document files so that you can modify the stuff, or data, that's in the files. You usually open document files by starting the application that created the document and then using that application's File Open command.

To use an application's File Open command, you usually follow a step sequence like that described below for opening a **Clipboard** file:

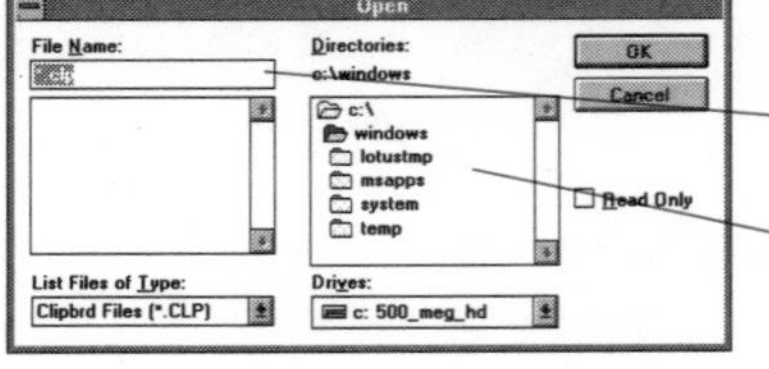

1. Choose the File Open command.
2. Enter the document file's filename.
3. If necessary, use the Directories and Drives list boxes to specify where the file is located.
4. Choose OK.

Opening Document Files with File Manager

If you double-click a document file listed in the File Manager directory window and **File Manager** knows which application created the document, File Manager opens the application and then tells it to open the document file. To tell File Manager which application created a document file, you choose the File Associate command to create an association.

Opening Document Files with a Program Item

Some applications let you specify which document file should be opened at the time you start the application. You may want to create **program items** that start an application and open a specific document file.

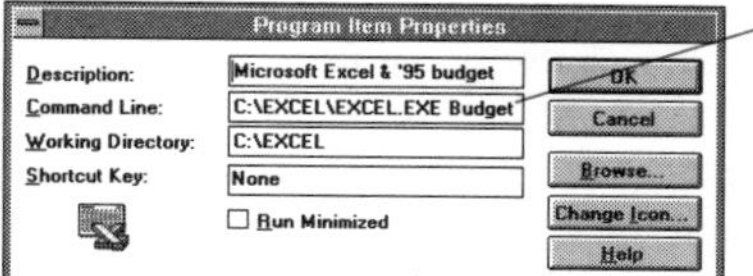

This command starts Microsoft Excel and opens the BUDGET.XLS document, or workbook, file. You can't see the XLS file extension because the text box isn't big enough. Trust me. It's there.

Saving Files

Option Buttons

Option buttons are sets of mutually exclusive choices. Sometimes option buttons are called radio buttons.

You can easily identify an option button set because it'll be a group of round buttons with a border. This is the **dialog box** that Windows displays when you choose the File New command to set up a new **group** or **program item.** It uses the New option button set to ask which new object you want to create.

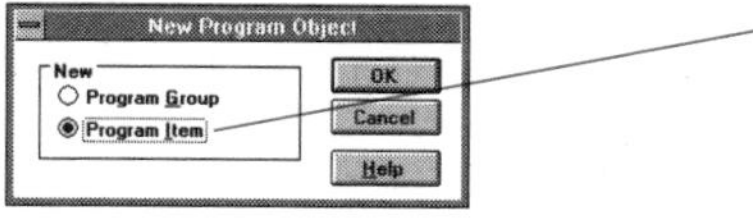

The selected option button will show a dot—called a bullet—in its center.

To choose one of the option buttons in a set, you click the button.

continues

Option Buttons *(continued)*

You can also use the keyboard. For example, you can use the Tab key to select the chosen button; press the Up and Down direction keys to highlight another button in the set and then press Enter. Or, if the option buttons in a set show underlined letters, you can also select an option button by pressing the Alt key and then the underlined letter. For example, you can select the Program Group button in the preceding option button set by pressing Alt+G.

Overtyping Normally, Windows-based **applications** insert the characters you type at the **insertion point.** You can often tell Windows-based applications to replace, or overtype, characters that follow the insertion point by pressing the Insert key. Any text you type will replace existing text, starting with the character just right of the insertion point. To turn off overtype, press the Insert key again.

Paintbrush The Paintbrush **accessory** lets you create, print, store, and manipulate **bit map** images.

 Program Manager >  Accessories >  Paintbrush

Creating a Bit Map Image

Once you start Paintbrush, you use Paintbrush tools to draw the lines and shapes and to add the colors that constitute the image.

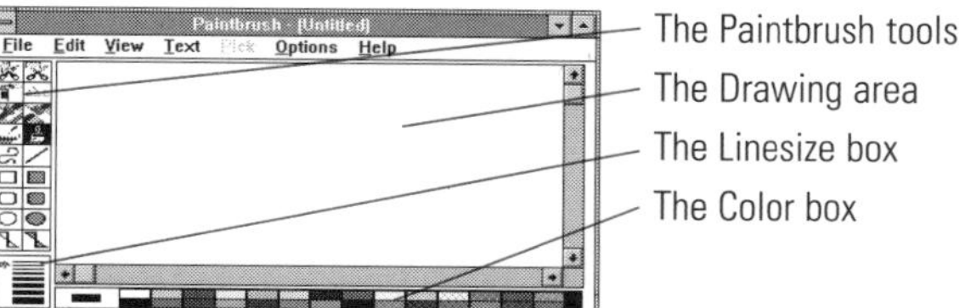

Using the Paintbrush Tools

To create bit map images, you use the Paintbrush tools.

Tool	Description
	Use the Scissors tool to draw a line (by dragging the mouse) around the image fragment you want to cut or copy. Then use the Edit Copy, Edit Cut, and Edit Paste commands to move the image fragment to and from the **Clipboard**.
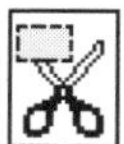	Use the Pick tool to draw a box (by dragging the mouse diagonally between its opposite corners) around the image fragment you want to cut or copy. Then use the Edit Copy, Edit Cut, and Edit Paste commands to move the image fragment to and from the Clipboard.
	Use the Airbrush tool to spray (by dragging the mouse) the selected colors on the image. To select the spray color, click one of the color boxes at the bottom of the Paintbrush **application window.** To select the spray thickness, click one of the linesize boxes in the bottom left corner of the application window. Then click the tool.
	Use the Text tool to add text to an image. To select the text color, click one of the color boxes. (Use the Text menu commands to control other features of the text.) Then click the tool.

continues

Paintbrush *(continued)*

Tool	Description
	Use the Color Eraser tool to erase (by dragging the mouse) the selected color. To select the color you want to erase, click one of the color boxes. To select the thickness of the eraserhead, click one of the linesize boxes. Then click the tool.
	Use the Eraser tool to erase (by dragging the mouse) all the colors in a portion of the image.
	Use the Paint Roller tool to color a shape (such as a box, a circle, or a polygon) or an image background. To color some shape or background, select the new color, click the tool, and then click the shape or background.
	Use the Brush tool to paint swaths of the selected color. To select the color, click one of the color boxes. To select the thickness of the brushstroke, click one of the linesize boxes in the bottom left corner of the application. Then click the tool.
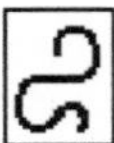	Use the Curve tool to draw a curved line of the selected color. To use this tool, first draw a straight line by dragging the mouse. Then curve the line by dragging it. To select the color, click one of the color boxes. To select the thickness of the line, click one of the linesize boxes. Then click the tool.
	Use the Line tool to draw (by dragging the mouse) a line of the selected color and thickness. Use the color and linesize boxes to specify the color and thickness.
	Use the Box tool to draw a rectangle (by dragging the mouse between the box's opposite corners). Use the color and linesize boxes to specify the box's border line color and thickness.
	Use the Filled Box tool to drag a rectangle (by dragging the mouse between the box's opposite corners). Use the color box to specify the box's interior, or fill, color.

Tool	Description
	Use the Rounded Box tool to draw a rectangle with rounded corners. This tool, as you no doubt guessed, works like the Box tool described earlier.
	Use the Filled Rounded Box tool to draw a filled rectangle with rounded corners. This tool works like the Fill Box tool. But you guessed this too, right?
	Use the Circle/Ellipse tool to draw circles and ovals (by dragging the mouse along the radius) of the selected color and using a line of the selected thickness.
	Use the Filled Circle/Ellipse tool to draw colored circles and ovals of the selected color. This tool works pretty much like its cousin, the Circle/Ellipse tool.
	Use the Polygon tool to draw a shape (by dragging and clicking the mouse) in the selected color and using a line of the selected thickness.
	Use the Filled Polygon tool to draw colored shapes in the selected color and using a line of the selected thickness.

Drawing squares and circles

To draw a square with one of the Box tools or a circle with one of the Circle/Ellipse tools, hold down the Shift key as you drag the mouse.

continues

Paintbrush *(continued)*

Printing an Image

Choose the File Print command to print the image. Graphic images are time-consuming to print, by the way. You may want to go get a cup of coffee.

Saving an Image

To save your image to disk, follow these steps:

1. Choose the File Save As command.
2. Enter a filename for the image. You don't enter a file extension. Paintbrush supplies the correct file extension for you, BMP. (BMP stands for bit map.)
3. Use the Directories and Drives list boxes to specify where the image should be located.
4. Choose OK.

Retrieving an Image

To retrieve an image you've previously stored on disk, start Paintbrush and then follow these steps:

1. Choose the File Open command.
2. Enter the image's filename.
3. If necessary, use the Directories and Drives list boxes to specify where the image is located.
4. Choose OK.

Opening Files; Saving Files

PIF

PIF is an acronym for Program Information File. A PIF lets you describe how an MS-DOS–based **application** you've decided to run under Windows should run. I'm not going to describe PIF files and how you create them here for three pretty simple reasons. First, you need to worry about PIFs only if you're running an MS-DOS–based application under Windows; so Windows-only users never need to worry about PIFs.

Second, Windows comes with PIFs for more than 200 popular MS-DOS–based applications. Even those Windows users who need or insist on using that favorite MS-DOS–based application probably won't need to worry about PIFs. The software company that sold the MS-DOS–based application almost certainly provided the PIF you need. (You get to the PIFs that Microsoft Windows provides by using the **Windows SetUp** program.)

Third, the whole thing is more work and more complicated than you want to wrestle with anyway. I promise you there are better things to do with your time. No joking.

Just so I don't keep you out in the cold, though, I want to leave you with one final thought. If you're ever milling around the coffee machine and somebody brings up the subject of PIFs, here's what you do: Squint, frown, and then say in a slightly disparaging tone, "Shoot, why are you still running MS-DOS–based applications?" Be sure, however, to walk away before the person answers. You don't want to get into a discussion of the difference between expanded and extended memory. Yuck.

PIF Editor

PIF Editor

The PIF Editor application lets you create and modify a **PIF,** or Program Information File. You probably won't ever need to use this application. So I won't describe it.

 Program Manager >  Main >  PIF Editor

Pointer The pointer is the arrow that moves across your screen as you roll the mouse across your desk.

Oh-oh. What's that? You don't have a mouse? OK. If you have some other kind of pointing device, such as a trackball, the pointer is the arrow that moves across your screen as you noodle around with this other, unidentified pointing device.

I should also mention that Windows-based **applications** will change what the pointer looks like as a secret signal to you about what they're doing. If a Windows-based application is busily working at some time-consuming task, the pointer may look like a tiny hourglass.

Points One point equals 1/72 inch. In Windows, you often specify sizes in points. **Fonts** get sized this way, for example.

Pop-up Box A pop-up box looks like a **message box,** but it doesn't have a **title bar** and it doesn't have a Control menu. **Help** uses pop-up boxes to display its **help glossary** definitions. **Character Map** uses pop-up boxes to display an enlarged picture of the selected character symbol.

Printing When you tell an application to print some **document**, what really happens is that the application creates a printable copy of the document (called a spool file in case you care) and then sends this printable copy to another application, **Print Manager**. Print Manager then prints the document.

Background Applications

Printers In Windows, you don't need to describe your printer or printers every time you install a new **application**. You just need to describe a printer once for Windows **Print Manager**. Print Manager does the work of printing.

You usually don't start Print Manager, although you can. A Windows-based application starts Print Manager when it's needed for printing.

Printers *(continued)*

Describing a New Printer

You can describe which printers you will use with Windows using either **Control Panel** or Print Manager. The steps for using either application are basically the same. Here are the steps for using Print Manager:

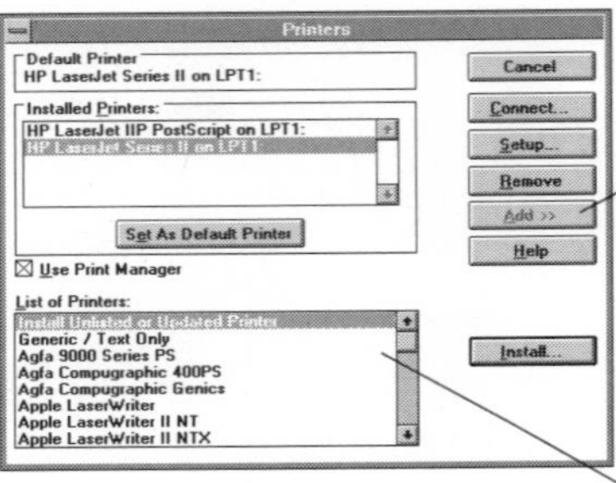

1 Start Print Manager; or if it's already active, switch to Print Manager using the Control menu's Switch To command.

2 Choose the Options Printer Setup command.

3 Choose the Add command button. Print Manager adds a list of printers to the bottom of the Printers dialog box and another command button, Install.

4 Select the new printer from the list and then click the Install command button.

5 If Windows asks, insert the appropriate Windows Setup disk and then choose OK.

Changing the Active Printer

If you install more than one printer, you can change which printer Windows uses. To do so, follow these steps:

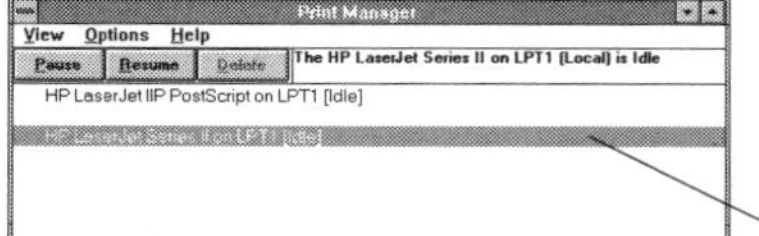

1 Start Print Manager; or if its already active, switch to Print Manager using the Control menu's Switch To command.

2 Double-click the installed printer you want to use.

3 Choose OK and close the Print Manager.

Changing the way a printer works

You can change the way a printer works by choosing the Options Printer Setup command, selecting the printer from the installed printer list, and then choosing the Setup command button. Windows displays a dialog box that lets you make whatever changes the printer allows.

Print Manager The Print Manager application collects the printable copies of **documents** that various **applications** send it, stacks them in a queue, and then, working as a **background application,** prints these documents one at a time.

Viewing the Queue

To view Print Manager's **print queue**, display Task List by pressing Ctrl+Esc; then switch to Print Manager by double-clicking its name.

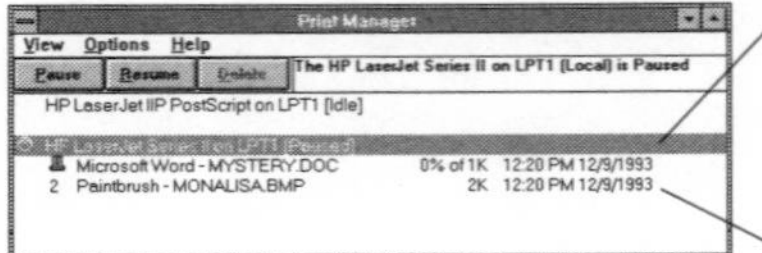

The Print Manager window lists the documents, or spool files, that it's busily printing.

You can change the order in which queued spool files print. Simply drag a print spool file ahead or backward in line.

Canceling a Printing Document

To tell Print Manager that it shouldn't print one of the documents listed in the print queue, select the document and then choose the Delete button.

Stopping and Starting Print Manager

You can use the Pause and Resume buttons to stop and start the printer. I'll let you guess which button does which action, OK?

Changing Print Manager's Speed

You can speed up, or accelerate, Print Manager by giving it a bigger share of your computer's processor time. To do this, switch to Print Manager, open the Options menu, and choose a higher priority. If the current priority is "low," choose the Medium Priority command. Or, if the current priority is "medium," choose the High Priority command. Note, though, that by increasing the Print Manager's priority, you'll slow down the other applications.

What Medium Priority means

When Print Manager works under the Medium Priority, Windows splits its time between Print Manager and your other Windows-based applications.

Print Queue The print queue is simply the list of print spool files that **Print Manager** is printing or is supposed to be printing.

Print Manager

Program Items Program items are simply the **icons** representing the applications in a **group**. Many icons for Microsoft **applications,** for example, get automatically thrown into the Microsoft Office group. For example, if you've installed Microsoft Excel and Microsoft Word and then you display the Microsoft Office group, you'll see program items for Excel and Word.

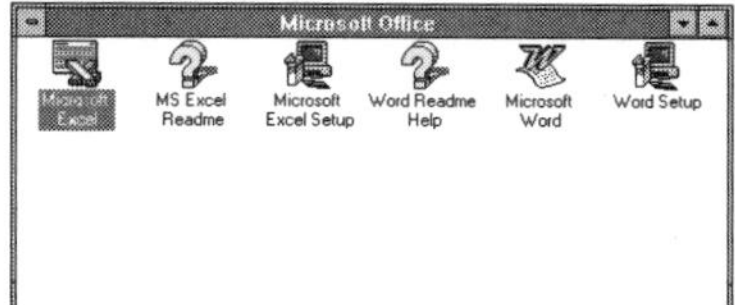

When you display a group window, you'll see program items, represented as **icons,** for each of the applications in the group.

Creating a Program Item

To create a program item for an application, follow these steps:

1. Display **Program Manager.**
2. Display the group window to which the item should be added.
3. Choose the File New command.
4. Mark the Program Item option button and press Enter.

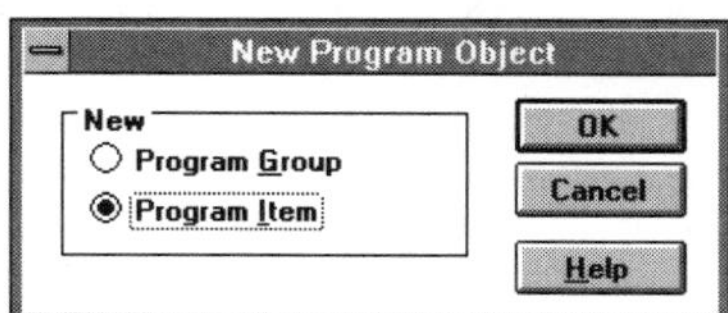

continues

Program Items *(continued)*

5 Enter a name for the program item in the Description text box.

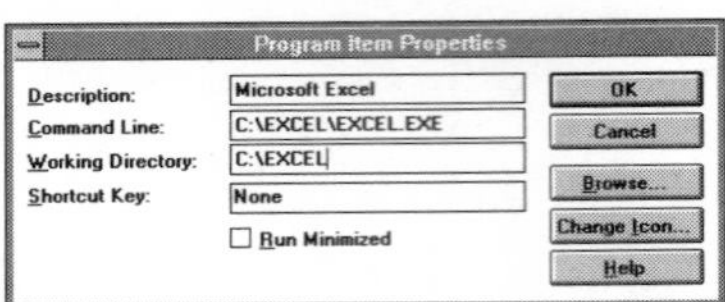

6 Enter the command that starts the application. The command probably includes the directory and the name of the program file. If you were adding a program item to start Microsoft Excel (which has the program file name EXCEL.EXE) and Microsoft Excel resides in the C:\EXCEL directory, you enter C:\EXCEL\EXCEL.EXE in the Command text box.

7 If an application looks for files in a certain directory, enter that directory's path in the Working Directory text box. Note too that if an application accepts additional parameters, such as the filename of the document you want opened when the application starts, you can include this information.

8 If you want to activate this program item's application with a keyboard combination, click on the Shortcut Key text box. Then press the keyboard combination. Your keyboard combination must include the Ctrl key, either the Alt or Shift key, and one other letter, number, or special character.

9 If this application should run in a **minimized window,** mark the Run Minimized check box.

10 Select the Change Icon command button to see examples of the application's icons that can be used to represent the application when it is minimized.

11 Press Enter.

Finding program files

If you have questions about the precise path or filename that should go into the Command text box, choose the Browse command button. Windows displays the Browse dialog box. It lists the files in the current directory and lets you change the current drive and directory by selecting entries from a list box. To select one of the listed program files, double-click it with the mouse or select it and then choose OK.

Deleting Program Items

To delete a program item, display its group, click the program item, and choose the File Delete command. When Program Manager asks you to confirm your deletion, choose OK. Note that this doesn't delete the program's application files.

Renaming a Program Item

To rename an program item, follow these steps:

1. Display Program Manager.
2. Select the program item
3. Choose the File Properties command.
4. When Program Manager displays the Program Item Properties dialog box, edit the contents of the Description text box.

Moving and Copying Program Items

You can move a program item to another group by dragging. You can copy a program item to another group by pressing Ctrl and dragging.

 **PIF Editor**

Program Manager Program Manager organizes your **applications** into **groups** and visually lists your applications as **program items.** It also offers the usual—although not the only—way to start your applications. (You can also use **File Manager**, for example.)

Protocol In the world of diplomacy, protocol refers to the rules of etiquette and ceremony that diplomats and heads of state follow. For example, "Don't drink from your finger bowl."

In the world of computers, protocol refers to the rules that two computers use to communicate. For example, "Don't send me data faster than I can receive it."

Terminal

Radio Buttons ⁘ Option Buttons

Readme Files

Software developers (such as Lotus Development) and hardware manufacturers (such as IBM or Compaq) often put late-breaking information in **Write** files and then create **program items** that start Write and load the file with the late-breaking information.

To get to this information, simply double-click the Write program item labeled "Readme."

Because a Readme file is a Write file, you can do with it what you do with any Write file: scroll through it, print it, add information to it, and so on.

Recorder

The Recorder **accessory** lets you create macros that repeat, or play back, keystrokes or mouse actions.

 Program Manager >  Accessories >  Recorder

---

Creating a Macro

To create a macro, follow these steps:

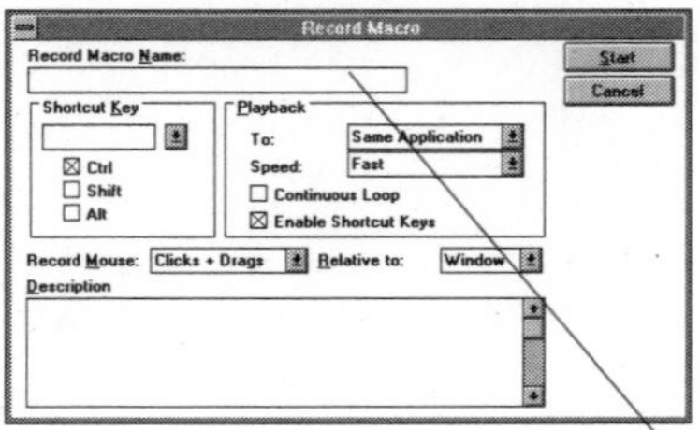

1. Position the **insertion point** at the place where the macro should begin recording keystrokes or mouse actions.
2. Switch to Recorder.
3. Choose the Macro Record command.
4. Specify a macro name or a shortcut key combination.

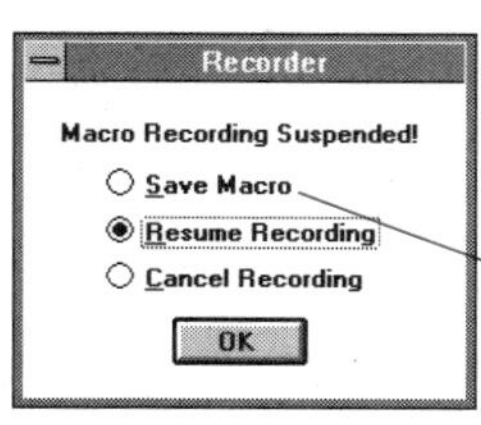

5. Choose the Start button. (Recorder returns you to the previous application.)
6. Do the hoodoo that you do so well. (In other words, perform the keystrokes and mouse clicks you want to record.)
7. Press Ctrl+Break.
8. When Recorder asks, select the Save Macro option and then choose OK. Congratulations. You're done. You've recorded a macro.

Controlling Recorder

The Record Macro dialog box lets you control how the Recorder records macros and plays them back. For example, you can exercise more control over the way Recorder records using the Record Mouse and Relative to drop-down list boxes. And you can control how and where the recorded macro plays back using the Playback To options.

Running a Macro

To run a macro, follow these steps:

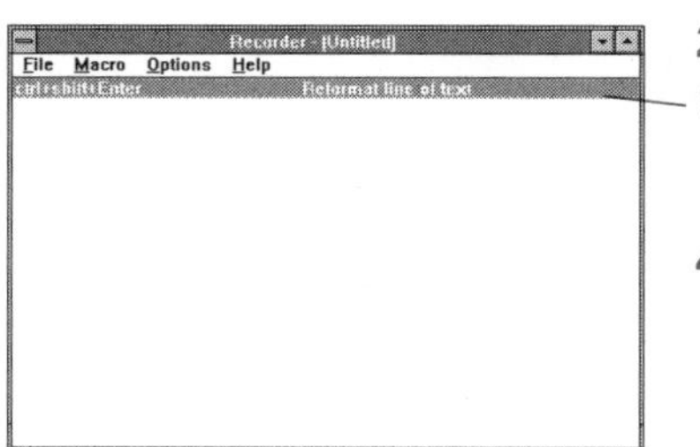

1. Position the insertion point at the place where the macro should begin repeating keystrokes or mouse actions.
2. Switch to Recorder.
3. Select the macro you want to run from the Recorder window.
4. Choose the Macro Run command. Congratulations. You're done. You've now run the macro you've just recorded.

continues

Recorder *(continued)*

Saving a Recorder File and Its Macros

To save your macros in a file on disk, switch to Recorder and follow these steps:

1. Choose the File Save As command.
2. Enter a filename for the macro. You don't enter a file extension. Recorder, ever helpful, supplies the correct file extension for you, REC.
3. Use the Directories and Drives list boxes to specify where the Recorder file full of useful macros should be located.
4. Choose OK.

Retrieving a Recorder File and Its Macros

To retrieve your macros file so that you can run one or more of the macros in it, start Recorder and then follow these steps:

1. Choose the File Open command.
2. Enter the Recorder file's filename.
3. If necessary, use the Directories and Drives list boxes to specify where the Recorder file is located.
4. Choose OK.

Opening Files; Saving Files

Renaming Files

Use **File Manager** to rename files.

 Program Manager >  Main >  File Manager

Renaming a File

To rename a file once you've started File Manager, follow these steps:

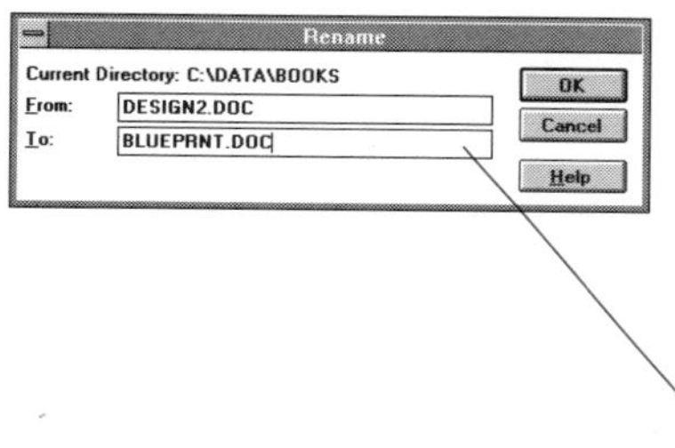

1. Click the **icon** of the disk drive that contains the file.
2. Click the directory and, if necessary, double-click the subdirectory that contains the file.
3. Select the file.
4. Choose the File Rename command.
5. Enter a new name for the file.
6. Choose OK.

File Names

Root Directory The root directory is the main directory that organizes a hard disk's directories and the files you don't place in another directory. If your hard disk drive is named C, for example, you can see the root directory's files and directories by typing starting **File Manager** and double-clicking on the C:>, or root directory, icon.

Saving Files You can almost always save the **document,** or file, that an **application** creates. You, for example, can save the workbooks that Microsoft Excel creates, the documents that WordPerfect creates, the appointment calendars that the Windows Calendar creates, and, well, you get the picture, right?

In general, you save the stuff shown in an **application window** or in an application window's **document windows** using the File Save As and File Save commands.

continues

Saving Files *(continued)*

Saving a File for the First Time

To save a file to disk for the first time, you follow these general steps:

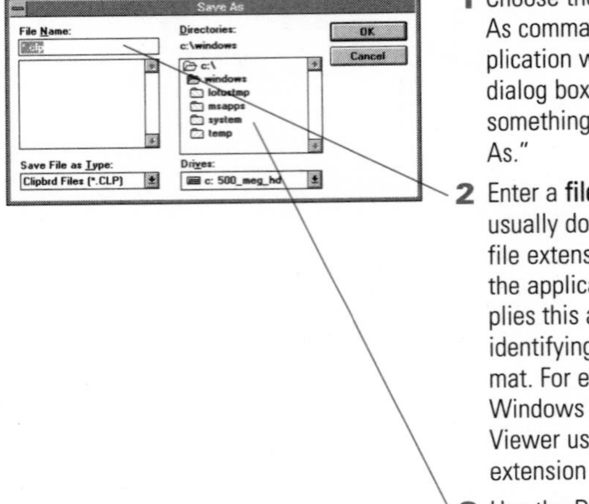

1. Choose the File Save As command. The application will display a dialog box named something like "Save As."
2. Enter a **filename.** You usually don't enter a file extension because the application supplies this as a way of identifying the file format. For example, the Windows Clipboard Viewer uses the file extension CLP.
3. Use the Directories and Drives list boxes to specify where the file should be located.
4. Choose OK.

Saving a File with a New Name or in a New Location

To save a file with a new name or in a new location, use the File Save As command as described in the preceding step sequence. Remember to specify the new name or location.

Resaving a File

To save a modified version of a file you've already saved once before, you choose the File Save command. When you do this, the application replaces the original, saved-to-disk file with what's in memory and displayed on your screen.

Screen Saver

Windows comes with a screen saver, which you turn on using **Control Panel**. A screen saver continually changes the picture shown on your screen so an image isn't permanently etched into your screen by being displayed too long.

Once you've started Control Panel, display the **desktop** settings. You can do this either by double-clicking the Desktop icon, which appears in the Control Panel window, or by choosing the Settings Desktop command. Either way, the Control Panel displays a **dialog box** that includes options for turning on a screen saver.

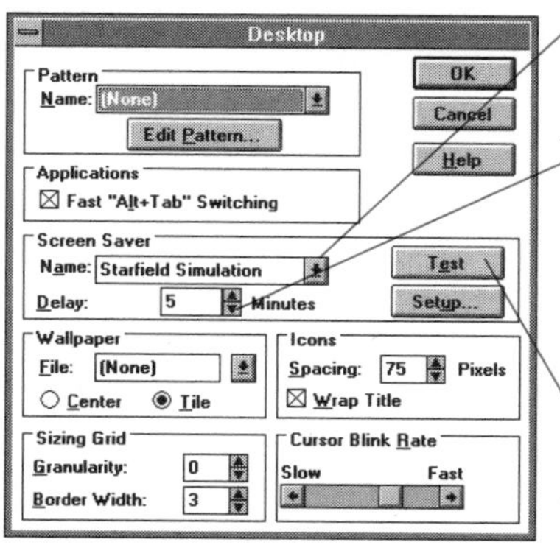

Use the Screen Saver Name **list box** to select a screen saver pattern.

Use the Delay text box to specify after how long a period of keyboard or mouse inactivity the screen saver should be turned on.

To see what your screen saver looks like, select the Test command button.

continues

Screen Saver *(continued)*

Once you've turned on the screen saver, Windows will display the screen saver image after the specified period of inactivity. To see the Windows **desktop** again and remove the screen saver, just move the mouse pointer or use the keyboard.

Assigning a password

If you select the Options command button, Windows lets you add a password that Windows requires before turning off the screen saver and redisplaying the Windows desktop. You might use a password to protect confidential information.

Wallpaper

Scroll Bars

Scroll bars let you move a document window's contents up and down and left and right. You do this, of course, because the document is too tall or too wide to fit entirely within its window.

Using the Mouse to Scroll

You can use the mouse on a scroll bar in a couple of ways:

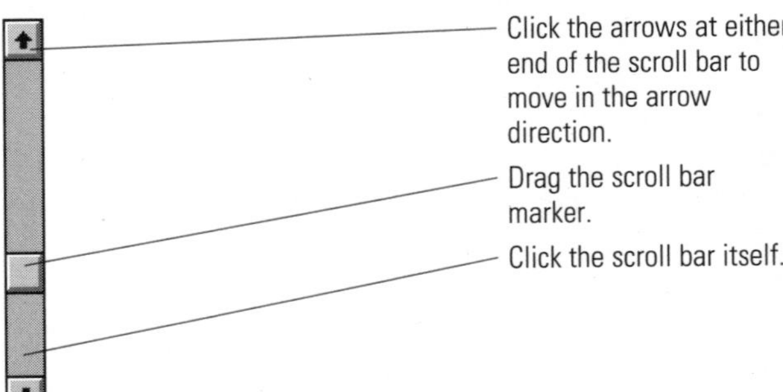

Scrolling

Scrolling simply refers to paging through a **document**. You can use the vertical or horizontal **scroll bars** if you've got a mouse. You can also use the PageUp and PageDown keys to scroll vertically, and you can press Ctrl+PageUp and Ctrl+PageDown to scroll horizontally.

Selecting

To change the contents of a text, list, or combo box or the setting of an option button or check box, you first need to select it. The easiest way to do this is by clicking the mouse. (In fact, if you don't have a mouse, your next best investment in computer hardware is a mouse.)

You can also select a box or a button on the active **dialog box** by pressing the Alt key and the underlined letter.

Selecting Text Box Contents

To select chunks of text in text boxes—including single characters—click in front of the first character and then drag the mouse to just following the last character.

Selection Cursor

The selection cursor is the thing that marks the selected option on a **dialog box** or the selected text in a box. OK. I know "thing" isn't a very specific noun. But how Windows marks **objects** with the selection cursor depends on the object being marked.

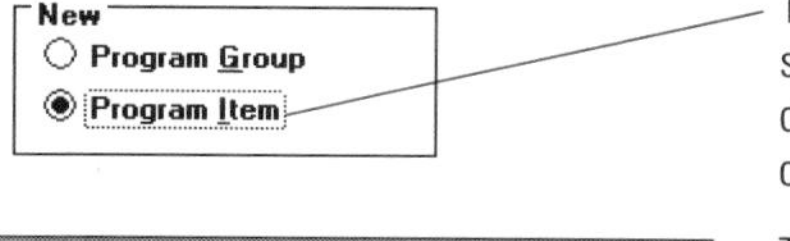

To mark a check box as selected, Windows draws a line around the check box.

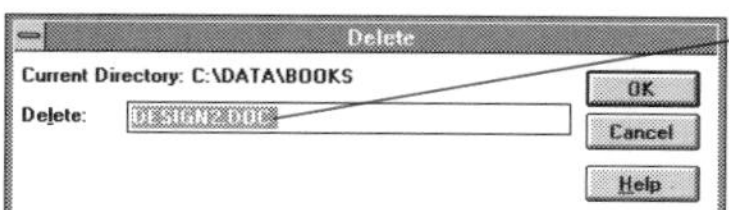

To mark a text box's contents as selected, Windows highlights the text.

Insertion Point

Sharing Data Among Applications You can easily share data amongWindows-based **applications.** You can move worksheets and charts you've created in Microsoft Excel or Lotus 1-2-3 to a word processor such as Microsoft Word or WordPerfect, for example. You can move values and chunks of text between other Windows-based applications—for example, from **Calculator** to an accounting program.

To share data among applications, you follow these general steps:

1. Select what you want to share: a worksheet range, a chart, a chunk of text, a value, or anything else.
2. Choose the application's Edit Copy command.
3. Switch to the other application using the Control menu's Switch To command.
4. Place the **insertion point** where you want to place the copied data.
5. Paste the contents of the **Clipboard** at the insertion point location. (Probably, you'll do so with that application's Edit Paste or Edit Paste Special command.)

To link or to embed—that is the question

When you choose Edit Paste Special to paste an object—a worksheet fragment, for example—into another application's document, you'll usually have a choice as to whether the pasted object is linked to the source document or is merely an embedded copy of the source document.

Drag-and-Drop; Object Linking and Embedding; Switching Tasks

Shortcut Menus A mostly cool new feature you're seeing in many Windows-based applications is the shortcut menu. Here's the scoop in case you don't already know. Many **applications** are now smart enough to know which **commands** make sense in which situations. Many applications also know which commands you, as a user, are most likely to use in those situations. If you want them to, many applications will display a **menu** of these commands—called the shortcut menu. All you need to do is click the right button on the mouse. (Remember that you use the left mouse button for selecting menus, commands, dialog box elements, and assorted and sundry items.)

Slider Button A slider button is actually just a scroll bar marker that, if dragged, doesn't scroll the contents of a **document window**. Instead, dragging the scroll bar marker tells a Windows-based application to adjust some setting or value.

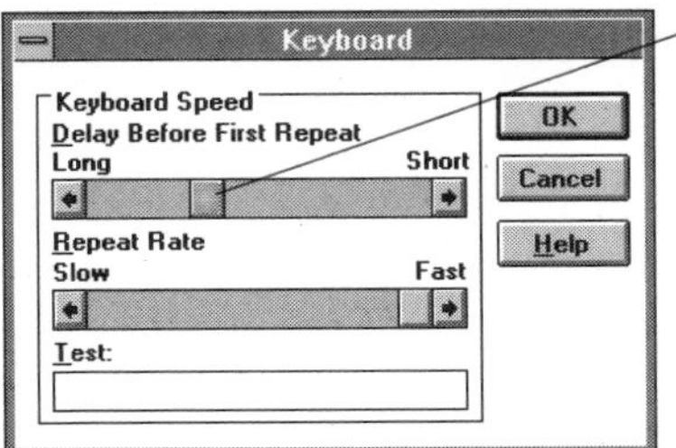

Adjusting this slider button changes the rate at which Windows repeats a character when you hold down a key. (You can display this **dialog box** on your screen by starting the **Control Panel** and choosing the Settings Keyboard command.)

Scroll Bars

SmartDrive MS-DOS comes with a disk-caching utility, SmartDrive, that works wonderfully with Windows. If you purchased your personal computer with MS-DOS and Windows, SmartDrive is almost certainly being started by your AUTOEXEC.BAT file. If SmartDrive isn't being started by your AUTOEXEC.BAT file when you boot your computer, you can probably add it yourself. Be sure, however, to carefully follow any directions provided in your MS-DOS user documentation.

Checking Your AUTOEXEC.BAT File

You can check your AUTOEXEC.BAT file to see if it's starting SmartDrive. The easiest way to do this if you're running Windows is to start **Notepad** and then open AUTOEXEC.BAT, which will probably be located in the root directory of drive C. If you see a line in the AUTOEXEC.BAT file that uses the filename SMARTDRV.EXE, your AUTOEXEC.BAT file is starting SmartDrive.

Monitoring the Effect of SmartDrive

If you acquired Windows version 3.1 and MS-DOS version 6 or later with your personal computer, you may be able to see information about how effective your SmartDrive disk caching is by starting SmartDrive Monitor.

Starting SmartDrive Monitor

You start SmartDrive Monitor in one of two ways. (Which way you start depends on how you installed MS-DOS version 6.) You may be able to start File Manager and choose the Tools SmartDrive Monitor command.

 Program Manager >  Main >  File Manager

Or you may be able to use the SmartDrive Monitor program item in the Microsoft Tools group.

 Program Manager >  Microsoft Tools > 

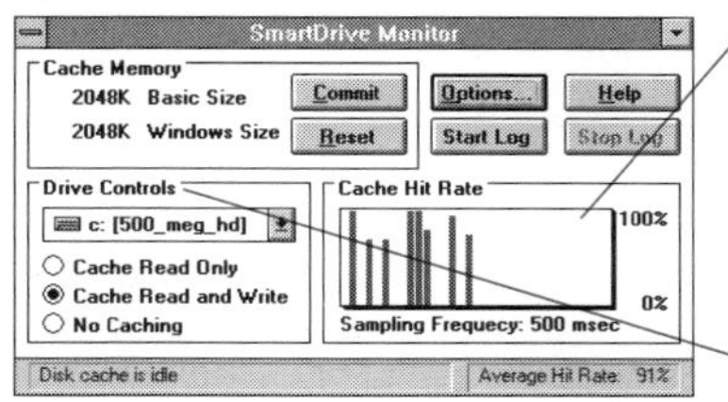

Use the Cache Hit Rate graph to tell how often your personal computer quickly grabs data from the disk cache in memory.

Use the Drive Controls options to tell which kind of disk caching SmartDrive performs and which disks it caches.

Sound Recorder You use the Windows Sound Recorder to play, record, and edit sound files. If you want to use this accessory, though, you'll need to have the appropriate sound hardware device, and you'll need to have it installed.

 Program Manager >  Accessories >  Sound Recorder

---

Standard Mode Mode

Starting Windows You start Windows by typing *win* at the **MS-DOS prompt.** If you don't want to see the copyright notice screen that Windows initially displays—let's say you know who owns the program—type *win* : at the MS-DOS prompt.

Starting Windows-Based Applications You start a Windows-based **application** either manually after you've started Windows or as part of starting Windows.

Starting an Application Manually

To start an application manually, follow these steps:

1. Start Windows by typing *win* at the **MS-DOS prompt.**
2. Display the group in which the application is a **program item.** For example, if an application's group is Microsoft Office, choose the Windows Microsoft Office command from the **Program Manager** menu bar.
3. Double-click the application's program item.

Starting an Application Automatically

To start an application each time Windows starts, follow these steps:

1. Start Windows—for example, by typing *win* at the MS-DOS prompt.
2. Display the group in which the application is a program item. For example, if the application's group is Microsoft Office, choose the Windows Microsoft Office command from the Program Manager menu bar.
3. Display the **StartUp group**—for example, by choosing the **Windows Startup** command from the Program Manager menu bar.
4. Drag the application's program item **icon** from the group window—such as Microsoft Office—to the StartUp group window to move the program item. Or, if you just want to duplicate the program item, hold down Ctrl while you drag.

StartUp Group The StartUp group is a group of **applications** in **Program Manager** that start automatically whenever you start Windows.

Starting Windows-Based Applications

Swap Files Windows creates a swap file when it wants to use a portion of your disk space as **virtual memory**. If you're running Windows in 386 enhanced mode, Windows automatically creates temporary swap files. (It also deletes these temporary swap files when you exit Windows.)

Choosing Swap File Type

The advantage of using a temporary swap file is that it occupies disk space only when you're running Windows. The disadvantage of a temporary swap file is that it isn't as fast as a permanent swap file. (Windows more carefully arranges permanent swap files on your disk.)

Creating a Permanent Swap File

To create a permanent swap file, first start **Control Panel.**

Once you've started Control Panel, follow these steps:

1. Double-click the 386 Enhanced **icon** or choose the Settings 386 Enhanced command.
2. Select the Virtual Memory command button when Control Panel displays the 386 Enhanced **dialog box.**
3. Select the Change command button when Control Panel displays the Virtual Memory dialog box.

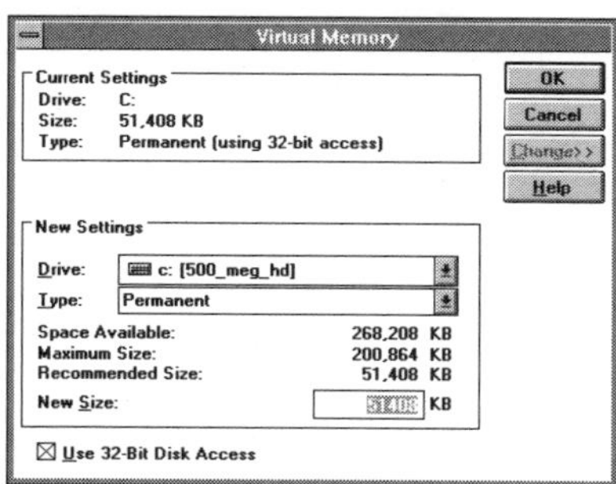

4. Activate the Type **drop-down list box** and select Permanent.
5. If necessary, limit the permanent swap file's size in the New size **text box** by specifying a size less than the Recommended Size listed in this dialog box.

continues

Swap Files *(continued)*

6. Verify that the Use 32-Bit Direct Disk Access check box is marked.
7. Choose OK.
8. When Control Panel asks if you want to make the Virtual Memory changes, choose Yes.
9. Choose OK to close the 386 Enhanced dialog box.
10. Exit from Control Panel.

Mode

Switching Tasks

To **multitask,** or run multiple **applications,** in the Windows operating environment, you use the Control menu's Switch To command. Selecting this command displays the Task List **dialog box,** which works as described below:

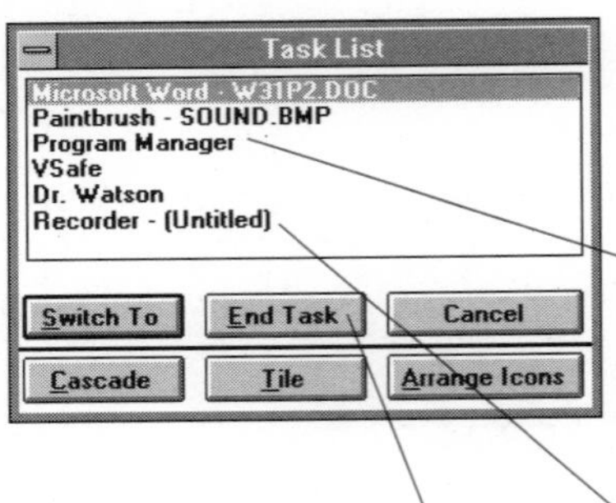

The Task List dialog box lists **Program Manager** as well as any other applications you or Windows has started.

To start a new application, double-click Program Manager. When Windows displays Program Manager, use it to start another application.

To switch to an application already running, double-click it. Or select it with the direction keys or the mouse and then choose Switch To.

Use the Cascade, Tile, and Arrange Icons command buttons to manage the **application windows** of the applications you've started.

You can use the End Task command button to stop a Windows-based application.

Easy Switching

You can cycle through the applications listed in the Task List dialog box using the keyboard. Press Alt+Tab to return to the last **active application**. Or hold down the Alt key and repeatedly press Tab to see **message boxes** that list the running applications, and release the Alt and Tab keys when the message box names the application you want to switch to. You can also press Alt+Esc to move through the open applications.

System Resources

People use the term *system resources* a couple of ways. One is a cool way to refer to all the stuff in your computer and all the gadgets connected to it. Another way that some people and, more important, that Windows uses the term *system resources* is to refer to three 64 KB chunks of memory, called local heaps, that Windows uses to go about its business.

Checking System Resources

You can check on your system resources by displaying **Program Manager** and then choosing its Help About Program Manager command.

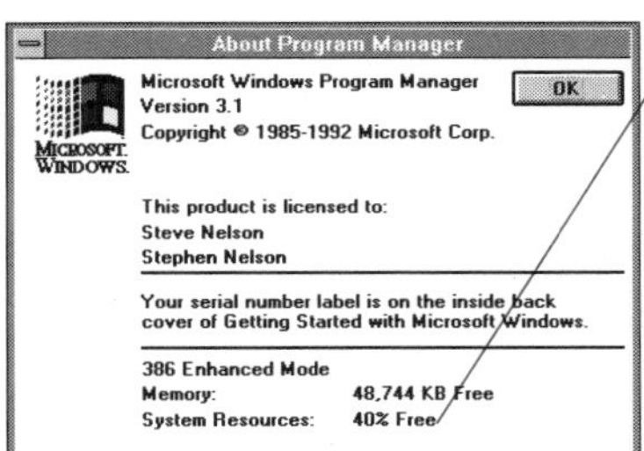

If your system resources percentage gets low—less than about 30%, say—you'll have trouble completing commands.

continues

System Resources *(continued)*

Freeing System Resources

If your system resources get low, you'll need to close an **application** or two or three. If that still doesn't work, close any unneeded Windows you've displayed—for example, **document windows.**

If neither of the preceding techniques works, it's very likely that one of the applications you've been running hasn't let go of its system resources memory. In this case, there's not much you can do about it except exit and then restart Windows. Sorry.

Out of Memory errors

If you've installed a lot of memory on your personal computer and you get an "out-of-memory" error, what you've run out of is probably system resources memory.

Switching Tasks

Task List

Task List shows whenever you choose the Switch To command from an application's Control menu. It lists **Program Manager** plus any additional **applications** that you or Windows has started.

You can use Task List to move another application to the foreground.

Background Applications; Foreground Applications; Switching Tasks

Terminal Terminal is the Windows communications **accessory.** With it and a modem, you can connect your computer to another computer, to an electronic mail service, and to many electronic bulletin board systems.

Once you start Terminal, you'll see the Terminal **application window** on your screen. If this is the first time you've used Terminal, you'll need at a minimum to enter the telephone number you want to call and describe the communications **protocol** that Terminal should use to connect to the other computer. You may also need to configure your modem.

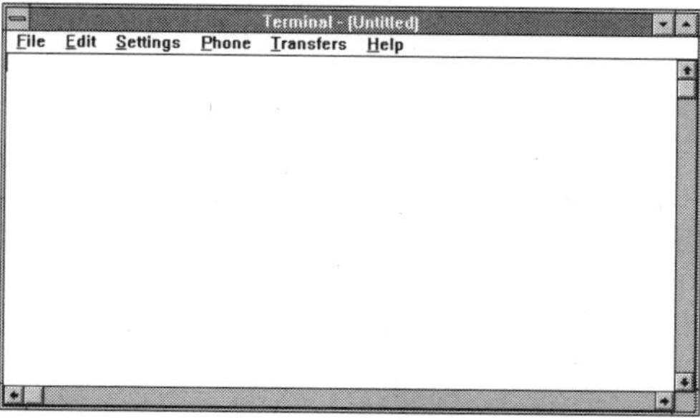

Entering the Telephone Number

Use the Settings Phone Number command to tell Terminal which telephone number your modem should dial. When you choose this command, Terminal displays a **dialog box** with a **text box** you use to give the telephone number.

continues

Terminal *(continued)*

Describing the Communications Protocol

Use the Settings Communications command to tell Terminal about the communications protocol. Typically, you should get the protocol—the rules for connecting to the other computer—from the electronic mail service, the bulletin board system, or the person who owns the computer you wish to connect to.

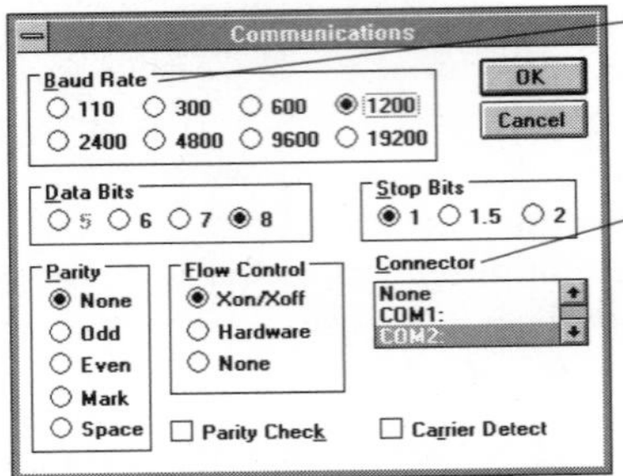

The Baud Rate option buttons tell Terminal how fast to transmit data.

The Connector list box tells Terminal which serial communications port you're using.

About the Data Bits, Stop Bits, Parity, and Flow Control settings

The other options in the Communications dialog box are important because they describe how the data is transmitted between your computer and the one you've connected to. You don't really need to understand the nitty gritty details of each setting, however. You just need to be sure that Terminal uses the same communications settings—the same protocol—as the computer that it connects to.

Configuring your Modem

If you're not using a Hayes-compatible modem, choose the Settings Modem Commands command. Then use the Modem Commands dialog box to tell Terminal which commands it needs to use to tell your modem to do things such as dial a telephone number and hang up the line.

Connecting to Another Computer

Once you've provided the telephone number and described the communications protocol, you're typically ready to connect to the other computer. To do this, choose the Phone Dial command. This tells Terminal to connect to the other computer. Once connected, you follow any instructions provided by the electronic mail service or bulletin board system.

Disconnecting from Another Computer

To disconnect from another computer, first complete any disconnection instructions provided by the electronic mail service or bulletin board system. Then choose the Phone Hangup command.

Saving Terminal Settings Information

You'll want to save the terminal settings changes you make using the Settings menu commands. To do so, follow these steps:

1. Choose the File Save As command.
2. Enter a filename for the terminal settings file. Don't enter a file extension. Terminal supplies the correct file extension for you, TRM.
3. Use the Directories and Drives list boxes to specify where the terminal settings file should be located.
4. Choose OK.

Retrieving Terminal Settings Information

To later use the terminal settings information, retrieve the file with the settings by following these steps:

1. Choose the File Open command.
2. Enter the terminal settings file's filename.
3. If necessary, use the Directories and Drives list boxes to specify where the file is located.
4. Choose OK.

continues

Terminal *(continued)*

Sending and Receiving Text Files

To move a text file—which is equivalent to telling Terminal to type in all the text in the file—choose the Transfers Send Text File command. Then use the Send Text File dialog box to identify the text file and give its location.

To capture the text that the other computer is sending and store it in a file, choose the Transfers Receive Text File command. Then use the Receive Text File dialog box to give a name to the new text file and specify a disk location.

If you send or receive text files and you have problems, you can use the Settings Text Transfers command to experiment with different text transmission methods. (Terminal, by default, uses something called Standard Flow Control, and it will probably work just fine.)

Sending and Receiving Binary Files

To move binary files (like **application** files) between your computer and the other computer with Terminal, use the Transfers Send Binary File and Transfers Receive Binary file commands. If you do send or receive binary files, use the Settings Binary Transfers command to tell Terminal which file-transfer protocol should be used: XModem/CRC or Kermit.

Opening Files; Saving Files

Text Box

A text box is simply an input blank you fill in by typing. To do this, select the text box such as by clicking; then start typing.

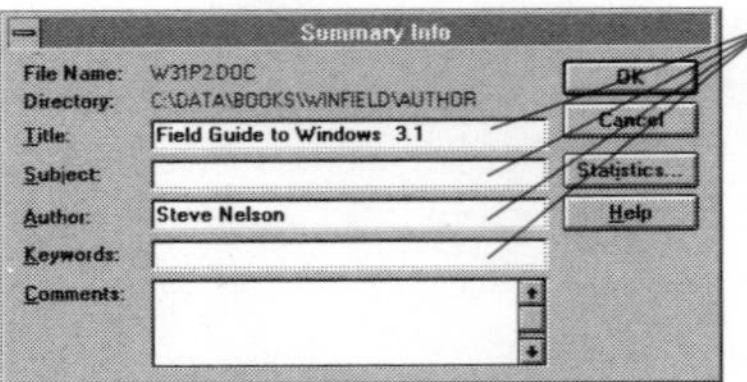

These input blanks, or boxes, are text boxes.

Deleting Characters

Position the **insertion point** by clicking or using the Left and Right direction keys. Use the Backspace key to erase the character preceding the insertion point; use the Del key to erase the character following the insertion point.

Replacing Text Box Contents

Position the insertion point at the beginning of the text box by clicking. Drag the mouse to the last character of the text box to select the entire text box contents. Then type the replacement text. What you type replaces the selected text.

Times

Dates and Times

Title Bars

Title bars identify the **application** running in an **application window** and the **document** displayed in a **document window.**

The title bars of the active application window and active document window usually show in a different color. Using the default Windows color palette, for example, the active window title bars are blue, and the inactive window title bars are white.

Toolbars

Toolbars are those rows of buttons and boxes, or tools, that sometimes appear at the top of your window just below the **menu bar.** Toolbar buttons provide shortcuts to common menu commands.

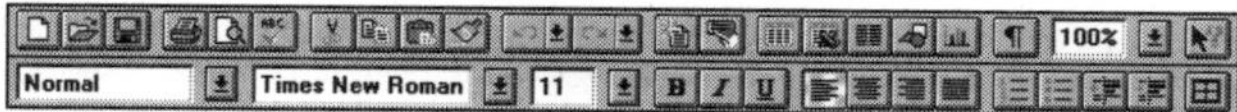

Microsoft Word, for example, initially displays two toolbars: the Standard toolbar and the Formatting toolbar.

TrueType TrueType is Microsoft Corporation's scalable font technology. If you're working with a Windows-based application, using TrueType **fonts** in your **documents** delivers two benefits. First, Windows and Microsoft Windows-based applications come with some cool TrueType fonts. (OK. Maybe that shouldn't count as a benefit, but you don't get any PostScript fonts with Windows or with Microsoft applications. PostScript is the competitive scalable font product.) Second, because of the way a scalable font is created, it's easy for Windows and Windows-based applications to change the **point** size in a way that results in legible fonts. Windows identifies TrueType fonts in the various Font list boxes with the TT prefix.

Adding fonts

If you purchase additional TrueType fonts, you can add them using Control Panel's Fonts setting.

Unerasing Files You should know that it may be possible to recover, or unerase, a document file. As long as you've got MS-DOS version 5 or later, you can unerase files. You may need to use the MS-DOS UNDELETE command. Or you may be able to use the Windows Undelete utility, which comes with MS-DOS version 6 and later.

Undeleting with Windows

Display the Microsoft Tools **group** and double-click the Undelete **program item**. When you see the Microsoft Undelete window, follow these steps:

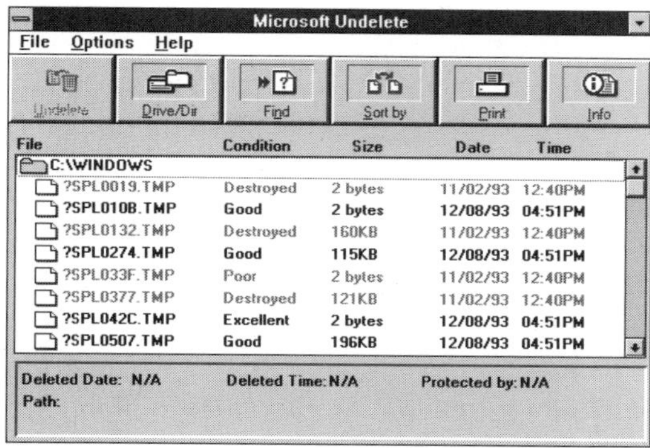

1 Click the Drive/Dir button.

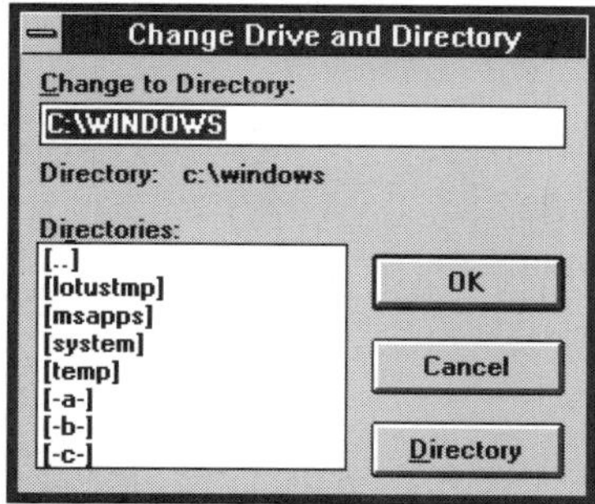

2 Specify the drive and directory in which the deleted file was stored; then choose OK.

3 If the file you want to undelete is listed in the window, click it.

4 Click the Undelete button.

5 When Microsoft Undelete prompts you, enter the first character of the deleted file name.

continues

Unerasing Files *(continued)*

Undeleting with MS-DOS

You can also use the MS-DOS UNDELETE command to undelete the previously deleted files. Here's the quick-and-dirty story on how to do so. Exit Windows so that you're at the MS-DOS prompt and make the directory in which the file used to be stored the active one. (Refer to the MS-DOS user documentation if you want help with this.) Then follow these steps:

1. Type the UNDELETE command followed by the file name and the extension—except substitute the question mark for the first letter in the file name. If you want to undelete the file named BUDGET94.XLS, for example, you type *UNDELETE ?UDGET94.XLS*.
2. If MS-DOS can find the deleted file in the active directory, it'll ask if you want to undelete ?UDGET94.XLS. Type *Y* for yes.
3. MS-DOS will ask you for the first letter in the file name. For example, if the deleted file's name was BUDGET94.XLS, you type *B*.

More about undeleting

There's more to undeleting files than I've described here. But let me point out a couple of things. First, when MS-DOS deletes a file, what it really does is erase the first letter in its list of file names. This is why it doesn't know the first character of the file name, supplies the question mark character instead, and asks you for the first character as part of undeleting the file. A second thing you should know is this: You can get much more fancy about undeleting files. You can tell MS-DOS to make a list of files you've deleted. (This way you don't have to remember the first letter in the file name.) And you can even tell MS-DOS that whenever it deletes a file it should make a backup copy of the file so that you can easily and successfully undelete the file later. (This of course is really the same thing as not deleting the file in the first place.) If you want to learn more about undeleting files, refer to your MS-DOS or Windows user documentation.

Virtual Memory Virtual memory simply refers to a computer's using disk space as **memory**. Windows uses virtual memory as long as it's running in 386 enhanced **mode**.

In Windows, what gets stored in the disk space doing double-duty as memory is something called a **swap file**.

Disk Caching; SmartDrive

Virus A virus is a program created by a pathetic little wimp with a bit of technical knowledge but zero maturity, zero common sense, and zero morals. The virus program this loser creates often attempts to destroy either your computer or the data stored on your computer's hard disk.

You get viruses by using infected floppy disks or infected software with your computer. If you only use software from reputable, professional software developers and you don't carelessly share floppy disks with all your computer friends, you don't have much to worry about when it comes to viruses.

If your machine does get a virus or you wonder if your machine has a virus, you can probably both locate and eradicate the virus using **Anti-Virus**, which comes with MS-DOS version 6 or later.

Wallpaper Windows lets you change the **desktop** pattern or wallpaper—the area that appears behind the windows of Windows—using **Control Panel.**

 Program Manager >  Main >  Control Panel

continues

Wallpaper *(continued)*

Changing the Desktop Pattern or Wallpaper

Once you've started Control Panel, display the desktop settings. You can do this either by double-clicking the Desktop **icon** or by choosing the Settings Desktop command. Either way, Control Panel displays a **dialog box** that includes options for changing the desktop wallpaper.

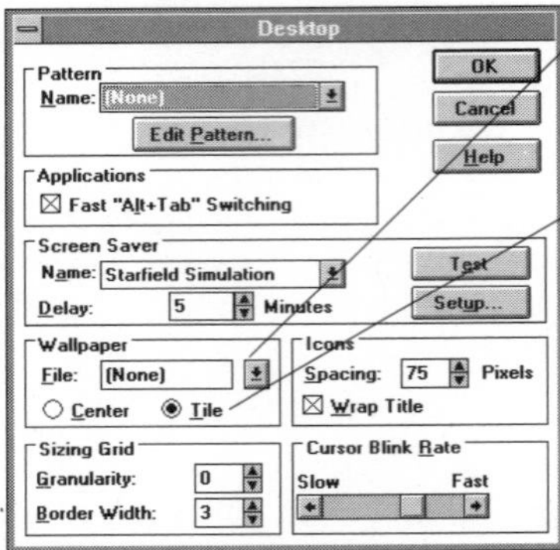

Use the Wallpaper File **drop-down list box** and select a wallpaper pattern.

Indicate whether the **desktop** should use the wallpaper pattern once to create the desktop background (indicated by Center) or should duplicate the wallpaper pattern—like the ceramic tiles in a bathroom (indicated by Tile).

If you don't use a wallpaper pattern

If you don't use a wallpaper pattern, Windows uses the Desktop Pattern setting for the desktop. If you're low on memory, by the way, you conserve memory by not using wallpaper.

Memory; Screen Saver

Wildcard Characters Wildcard characters stand for other characters in an expression. For example, you might use wildcard characters as part of specifying the **filename** you enter in a **dialog box.** The most common wildcard characters are the ? and * symbols. A ? can stand for any single character. An * can stand for any single character or any group of characters. If this sounds like something you want to learn more about, refer to the MS-DOS user documentation.

Wild Characters Wild characters are simply house guests that arrive unannounced, open bags of potato chips without asking, and then drink all the beer in your refrigerator. Don't confuse these unsavory folks with the useful-but-similarly-entitled tool, **Wildcard Characters.**

Window Buttons Arranged around the outside edge of the application and document windows—such as the Microsoft Word **application window** and the **document windows** shown below—are buttons. You can use these buttons to display the Control menu, to close windows, and to minimize and change window size.

continues

Window Buttons *(continued)*

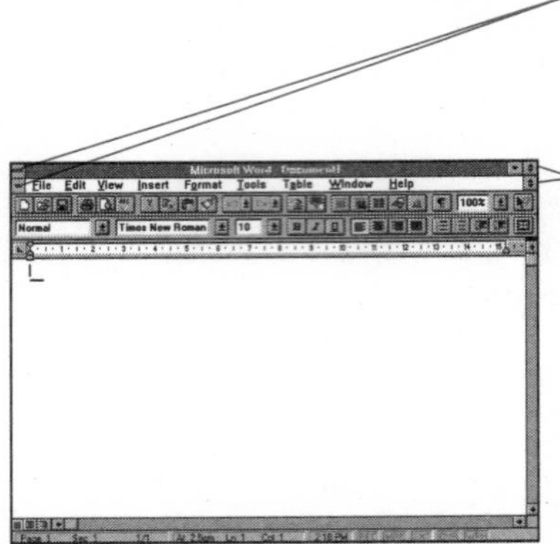

Click these buttons, called the Control-menu **icons,** to display a window's Control menu.

Click these buttons to minimize a window so that it appears only as an **icon.** (Minimized document windows appear as icons at the bottom of the application window.)

The Maximize/Restore buttons' appearance depends on the window size. If a window isn't maximized, click the button that looks like an upward-pointing arrowhead to maximize. If a window is maximized, click the button that looks like a double-headed arrow to restore a window to its usual, unmaximized size.

A quick exit

You can close a document window by double-clicking its Control-menu box. You can close an application window by double-clicking its Control-menu box.

Window Panes In some applications, you can split a **document window** into panes and then use the panes to view different portions of the same **document**. You might do this to view a word processor document's table of contents from page 1 in one pane and something from the fifth section of the document from page 21 in another pane.

The way you create panes depends on the application, but the rules are fairly straightforward if you're working with a Microsoft application.

Creating Window Panes

Follow these steps to split a window into panes in a Microsoft application such as Word or Excel:

1. Choose the Window Split command to split the **active document** window into two panes. To show the split window, an application often displays a fuzzy, thick horizontal line through the middle of the **document window.**
2. Use the mouse or the Up and Down direction keys to move this "pane-splitting" line to the place you want the window split.
3. Press Enter or click the mouse to anchor the pane line.

Removing Window Panes

To remove a window pane in a Microsoft application such as Word or Excel, choose the Window Remove Split command. (This command replaces the Window Split command once you've split a window into panes.)

Jumping Between Window Panes

You can move the **insertion point** between window panes by clicking in one or the other.

Windows NT Windows NT is the most powerful version of the Windows operating system family, so chances are you won't need it. With Windows NT, you don't need MS-DOS. With Windows NT, you get the same sorts of system security measures you do with a big computer system. Finally, with Windows NT, your computer can access monstrously huge chunks of memory (as much as 4 gigabytes) and even more monstrously huge chunks of disk space (as much as 16 billion gigabytes). Yikes.

Windows for Workgroups

Windows Setup The Windows Setup application adds **program items** for Windows–based applications and for MS-DOS–based applications. It also lets you remove unneeded files from your hard disk and change system settings.

Adding a Single Application

To add a **program item** for an **application** (and, in the case of an MS-DOS–based application, create **PIF** files), start the Windows Setup application and then follow these steps:

1. Choose the Options Set Up Applications command.
2. When Windows asks, indicate that you want to set up a single application; then choose OK.
3. When Windows asks, give the path and file name for the application.
4. Choose a **group** into which the new program item should be placed.

Adding Multiple Applications

To add program items for multiple applications (and, in the case of MS-DOS–based applications, create a PIF), start the Windows Setup application and then follow these steps:

1. Choose the Options Set Up Applications command.
2. When Windows asks, indicate that you want to search the hard disk for applications; then choose OK.
3. When Windows asks, indicate where it should search. (You may specify your entire hard disk.) Then choose OK. Windows Setup begins searching for application files. As it finds them, it builds a list.
4. When Windows asks via the Add Applications **dialog box,** select the applications for which you want to add program items and then click the Add command button.
5. Choose OK. Windows Setup then creates a new group named Applications and adds the new program items to it.

Removing Unneeded Files

You can use the Options Add/Remove Windows Components commands to remove unneeded files. When you choose this command, Windows Setup displays a dialog box that contains **check boxes** corresponding to various categories of potentially unneeded files. To remove a category of unneeded files, unmark the check box and choose OK.

If you make a mistake and later need to add back a category of files, choose the Options Add/Remove Windows Components commands and mark the check box. Windows Setup will prompt you to enter one (or more) of the Windows Setup disks.

Deleting specific files

If you don't want to delete an entire category of files but do want to delete specific files, choose the Select Files command button to the right of the check box. Windows Setup displays a list box of specific files. You click the file and then the Remove command button.

continues

Windows Setup *(continued)*

Changing System Settings

Use the Options Change System Settings command to describe or replace your display (monitor), keyboard, mouse, or network. When you choose this command, Windows Setup displays a dialog box with four **drop-down list boxes**—one for each of the four system settings. To make a change, you simply activate the appropriate list box and select one of its entries.

Windows for Workgroups

Windows for Workgroups is another member of the Windows operating system family. What differentiates Windows for Workgroups from Windows is that it lets you connect personal computers in what's called a peer-to-peer network as long as each of the computers in the network runs Windows for Workgroups and has a special communications device called an ethernet card.

Word Wrap

Word wrap simply means that a word processor such as **Write** or **Notepad** moves the **insertion point** to the next line once you run out of room on the current line and also moves big words to the next line if the move makes things fit better.

Write

The Write **accessory** is a simple word processor. If you don't have another word processor, you should be able to use Write to do most of your writing as long as the **documents** you want to produce aren't too complicated or fancy.

Starting Write

Start Write by displaying the Accessories **group** and then double-clicking the Write **program item**.

Creating a Document

To enter text into a document, you simply use the keyboard to type the **characters**. Tap, tap, tap. No joke. That's all there is to it.

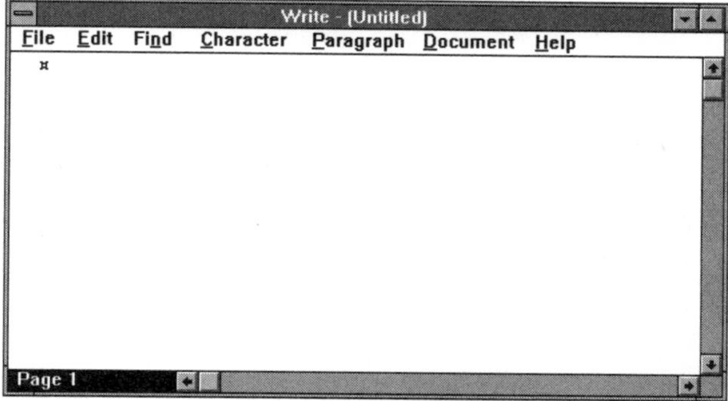

Don't press the Return key at the ends of lines; Write moves the **insertion point** to the next line when it runs out of room. Write also moves words from one line to the next line if there isn't room.

To edit text you've already entered, first select the character or block of text you want to change. (You can do this by clicking just before the first character you want to change and then dragging the mouse to just after the last character you want to change.) Next type the new text that you want to replace the old text.

You can erase the preceding character by pressing Backspace.

You can erase the current selection—a character, a sentence, a picture, or a paragraph —by pressing the Del key.

continues

Write *(continued)*

Finding and Replacing Text

Use the Find Find command to locate text within a document.

Use the Find Replace command to find text within a document and then replace it.

If you want to find characters that don't appear on the keyboard, use one of these character codes:

Code	What it represents
?	Any single character—for example, if you search for the two-character string I?, Write would find "it", "if", "is", and so on.
^w	The space character—for example, the space between two words.
^t	The tab character—for example, the tab that indents a paragraph's first line.
^p	The end-of-paragraph character.
^d	The manual page break.

Formatting a Document

Use the Character menu commands to **bold** or *italicize* characters and to change character **fonts**.

Use the Paragraph menu commands to change alignment, indention, and line spacing.

Use the Document menu commands to add headers and footers to the document, to set tab stops, and to control page layout.

Adding a Picture to a Document

You can add **bit map** pictures to a Write document—for example, a bit map picture you created in **Paintbrush**. To do this, follow these steps:

1. Copy the picture to the **Clipboard.**
2. Switch to Write.
3. Open the document.
4. Position the insertion point.
5. Choose the Edit Paste or Edit Paste Link command to place the bit map picture stored on the Clipboard into the Write document.

Printing a Document

Choose the File Print command to print the Write document.

Saving a Write Document

To save your document to disk, follow these steps:

1. Choose the File Save As command.
2. Enter a filename for the document. You don't enter a file extension. Write supplies the correct file extension for you, WRI.
3. Use the Directories and Drives list boxes to specify where the document file should be located.
4. Choose OK.

Retrieving a Write Document

To retrieve a document you've previously stored on disk, start Write and then follow these steps:

1. Choose the File Open command.
2. Enter the document's file name.
3. If necessary, use the Directories and Drives list boxes to specify where the document is located.
4. Choose OK.

Why get a word processor?

Write comes with Windows, you're thinking to yourself. Hmmm. Why go out and spend good money on an expensive word processor? Good question. In truth, you may not need to if you don't do much writing and if the documents you want to produce are pretty simple: letters home to Mom, say. Or a quick memo every now and then. But you should know that what a program such as Microsoft Word, WordPerfect, or Lotus AmiPro offers is far more than what Write offers. All the real, live word processors are faster, do more, and do it better. And they also all provide tools to make it easier to write and to produce professional-looking documents.

Opening Files; Saving Files

TROUBLE-SHOOTING

Got a problem? Starting on the next page are solutions to the problems that plague new users of Microsoft Windows. You'll be on your way—and safely out of danger—in no time.

PRINTING

You Want to Cancel a Printing Document

If you've told an application to print a document and you later realize you don't want to print, you may want to cancel the printing. This is particularly true if the document is long and you'd really prefer not to waste the paper.

Switch to Print Manager and delete the job

When Windows-based applications print documents, they usually create print spool files and then send these print spool files to the Windows **Print Manager.** Print Manager then does the **printing.**

To cancel a printing document once it's been sent to Print Manager, you need to follow these steps:

1. Choose the active application's Control-menu Switch To command by pressing Ctrl+Esc.
2. Select Print Manager from the Task List dialog box by double-clicking.
3. Click the printing document.
4. Click Print Manager's Delete command button.

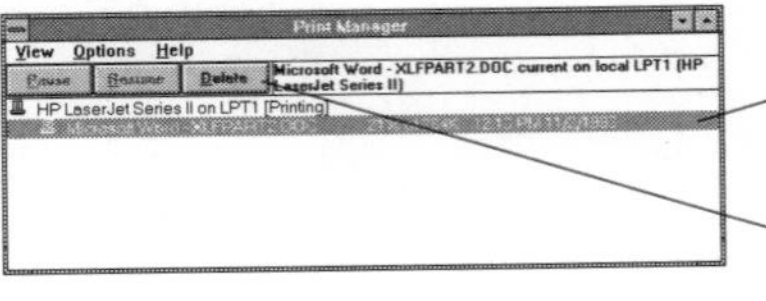

Control-Menu Commands; Printing; Switching Tasks

FILES

You Can't Save a Document, or File

Windows-based applications need a certain amount of **system resources** (basically, special chunks of **memory**) to save a document. If your system resources get too low, therefore, you can run into some pretty serious problems. Fortunately, as long as you keep your cool, this doesn't have to be a disaster. Your basic tack is a simple one. You want to free up system resources and then try again to save the document.

Close your other open applications

Switch to any of your other open applications and close them. You can switch to the other open applications by choosing the active application's Control-menu Switch To command, selecting the other application from the Task List dialog box, and pressing Enter.

Once you've closed all the other applications, return to the application with the unsaved document and try to resave it.

If you're the superstitious sort, go ahead and cross your fingers. It won't make any difference, but it may make you feel better.

Try opening another session of the application

If you've closed all the other open Windows-based applications and still can't save the document, you can try starting a second copy of the application, copying the document to it (using the **Clipboard**), and then saving the document. This may work because in some cases, even though you've freed up system resources, an application that's already running can't use those resources. (Weird, huh?) A newly started application, however, may be able to use the resources. So here's what you can do:

continues

You Can't Save a Document, or File *(continued)*

1. Copy the unsavable document to the Clipboard by selecting the entire document and choosing Edit Copy.
2. Start a second copy of the application. (Refer to the Windows A to Z entry **Switching Tasks** if this isn't something you know how to do right off the top of your head.)
3. Paste the Clipboard contents into the new document by choosing Edit Paste.
4. Save the new document using a new filename.

Saving Files

You Can't Find a Document, or File

Sure, this is a bummer. But a lost document, or file, doesn't have to be as big a problem as you think.

Use File Manager's File Search command

You can usually use File Manager's File Search command to locate lost files. When you choose the command, **File Manager** displays the Search dialog box.

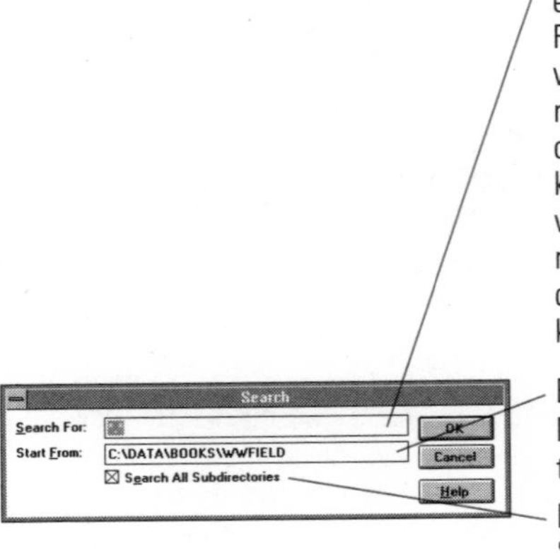

Enter the filename and extension in the Search For text box. Use the ? wildcard character to represent single characters you don't know, and use the * wildcard character to represent any set of characters you don't know.

Enter the path that File Manager should search in the Start From text box.

Mark the Search All Subdirectories check box if you do want to search them. If you want to search your entire hard disk, specify the **root directory.**

You Accidentally Erased a File

If you've just erased a file that you now realize you desperately need, stop what you're doing. Don't save anything else to your hard disk.

Unerase the File

Turn to **Unerasing Files** in the Windows A to Z section and follow its instructions for unerasing a file. Good luck, James.

Opening Files; Saving Files

DISKS

Your Hard Disk Is Full

If your hard disk begins to fill up, you'll either want to free up some space or buy a bigger disk—for two reasons. First, Windows needs a certain amount of free disk space just to run (unless you've created a permanent **swap file**). Second, some Windows-based applications go, like, totally berserk if they encounter a full hard disk. (By "totally berserk," I just mean you'll get an **application error.**)

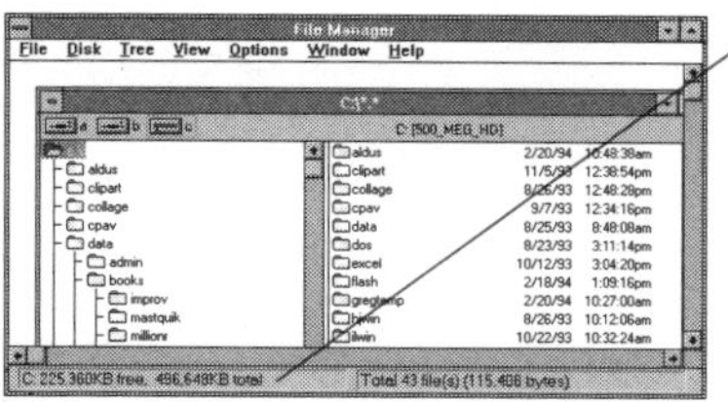

Check your free disk space by starting **File Manager**, selecting the hard disk's **root directory,** and then reading the status bar.

continues

Your Hard Disk is Full *(continued)*

Erase any unneeded files

The most direct way to free up disk space is to remove individual files from the disk using File Manager's File Delete command. If you want to save the files, you can first copy them to a floppy disk.

In general it's not a good idea to remove files you didn't create in the first place. It may be, for example, that you and Windows or you and some application have different ideas as to whether a file is needed.

If you're the adventurous sort

One possible exception that I feel uncomfortable even bringing up concerns files with the extension TMP. The TMP extension usually means that a file is temporary. And temporary usually means "not permanent" and "of passing importance." So, usually, you can erase files with the TMP extension without much risk. *Please, please, please* don't do this without thoroughly checking the user documentation for the applications you use. Who knows? Maybe some geek has decided that TMP no longer means "temporary."

Use Windows Setup to remove extra baggage

You can use the **Windows Setup** application to remove programs (such as the Windows accessories you don't need), Readme files you don't read, and some of the little extra stuff that hangs around on disk and consumes space (such as the bit map images).

Use disk compression

MS-DOS versions 6 and later come with a disk compression utility, **DoubleSpace.** You may want to use DoubleSpace to scrunch more data on your disk. For more information on DoubleSpace, refer to the MS-DOS user documentation.

Change the way UNDELETE works

How you use the UNDELETE command that comes with MS-DOS versions 5 and later can dramatically affect how quickly you fill up your hard disk. Here's why: You can tell the UNDELETE command to use its Delete Sentry option, in which case it makes a copy of files you delete just in case you later want to undelete one.

You may want to check on the UNDELETE options you've chosen. If you're using the Delete Sentry option, you may want to weigh the extra security it provides (in terms of recovering deleted files) with the high cost in hard disk usage.

For more information on UNDELETE, refer to the MS-DOS user documentation.

 **Copying Files; Erasing Files; Unerasing Files**

You Can't Save a File to a Floppy Disk

If you attempt to save a file or copy a file to a floppy disk but can't, there are several things you can try.

Unprotect the floppy disk

If you get a message that says a disk is write-protected, you won't be able to save a file, or write, to the disk until you unprotect the disk.

To write to a 5.25-inch floppy disk, verify that the floppy disk has a notch. If a piece of tape or an adhesive tab is covering up this notch, you won't be able to write anything to the disk. To unprotect the floppy disk, remove the tape or adhesive tab covering the notch.

To write to a 3.5-inch floppy disk, verify that there is no square hole in the disk's top right corner when you're holding the disk so you can read its label. If there is a square hole, flip the floppy disk over, and move the slide so that it covers the hole.

Why the write-protection?

I don't mean to sound like a worrier, but before you decide it's OK to write to a previously write-protected floppy disk, you may want to consider the reasons someone protected the disk. Who knows? Maybe there's stuff on the disk that shouldn't be written over.

continues

You Can't Save a File to a Floppy Disk *(continued)*

Format the floppy if needed

If you get a message that a Windows-based application such as File Manager can't read a disk, it may be because the disk isn't formatted. If you know this is the case or you know there's nothing on the floppy disk that you or the person in the next cubicle needs, you can format the floppy disk. (For practical purposes, formatting a disk destroys everything that's on it.)

Formatting Floppies

WINDOWS AND APPLICATIONS

You Can't Find an Application Window

If you've started more than one application, and particularly if you display applications in large or maximized windows, you may temporarily lose track of background applications.

Click the background application

If you can see a background application's window, you can move it to the foreground by clicking it.

Tile the application windows

If you want to see all the unminimized application windows at the same time, display **Task List** by pressing Ctrl+Esc and choose the Tile button.

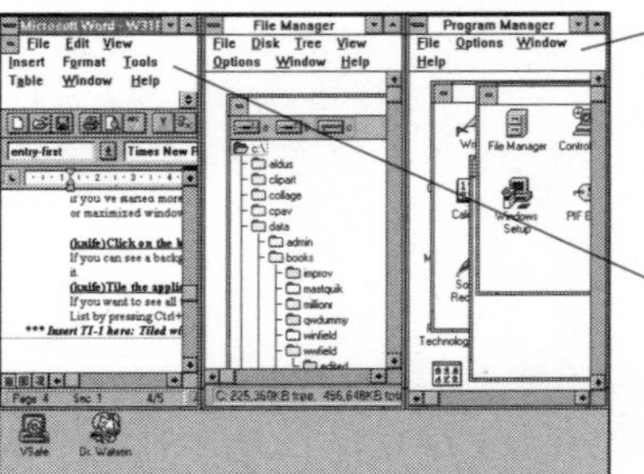

These are "tiled" **application windows.** Windows doesn't tile minimized application windows.

Here's a curious tidbit. When Windows resizes an application window by tiling, it may split the application's **menus** into two or more bars.

Cascade the application windows

If you want to see the **title bars** of all the unminimized application windows, display Task List by pressing Ctrl+Esc and choose the Cascade button.

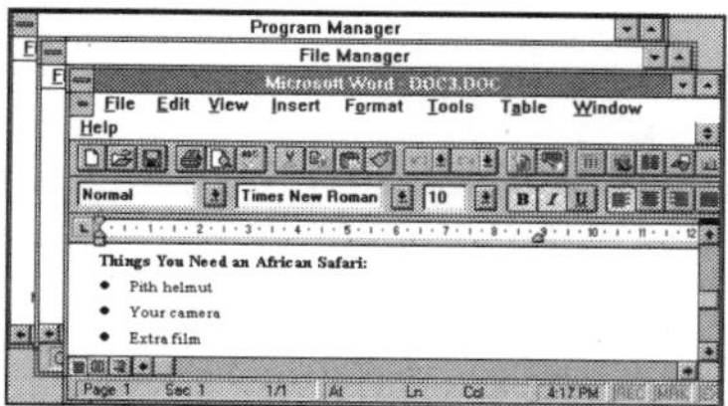

I "cascaded" these application windows. You're wondering if "cascaded" is really a verb. Yes, it is. I just spell-checked it.

Moving between applications

If you tile or cascade application windows, you can move an application to the foreground by clicking some part of its window—for example, its title bar.

You've Started More Than One Copy of an Application

If you begin **multitasking** with the Control menu's Switch To command, it's not all that difficult to find that you've started multiple copies of a single **application.** This consumes **system resources** and **memory.** And it makes it difficult to share data across **documents.**

Exit from the active duplicate application

If one of the duplicate application tasks is active—say you've got two copies of Microsoft Word running—you can exit from it. (Do this with the File Exit command.) This closes the active Word task, but the other inactive Word task will still be open, or running.

continues

You've Started More Than One Copy of an Application *(continued)*

Close one of the duplicate tasks

If another application or **Program Manager** is active, follow these steps to close the second, extra Word task:

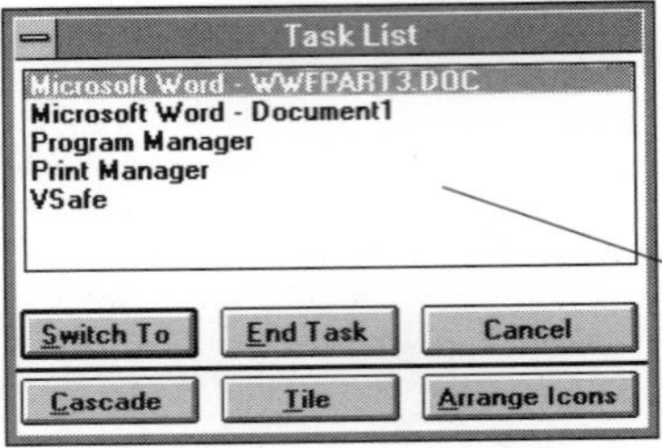

1 Choose the application's Control-menu Switch To command—for example, by pressing Ctrl+Esc.

2 Select one of the duplicate applications from the Task List dialog box and choose the Switch To command button.

3 When the application window appears, choose the File Exit command.

 **Control-Menu Commands; Switching Tasks**

You Can't Get an Application to Respond

It's unlikely but still possible that a bug in the foreground application (or a bug in a background application) will cause an application to stop responding. If this happens, you won't be able to choose menu commands. And you may not be able to move the mouse pointer.

Terminate the unresponsive application

Unfortunately, if an application truly is unresponsive, if it ignores your keyboard and mouse actions, there's nothing you can do to make it start responding again. When this is the case, however, you can press Ctrl+Alt+Delete.

Ctrl+Alt+Delete—you press the three keys simultaneously—tells Windows to look at the active application and check for responsiveness. Windows makes this check and displays a message that tells you whether the application is, in fact, unresponsive.

```
This Windows application has stopped responding to the system.

*   Press ESC to cancel and return to Windows.
*   Press ENTER to close this application that is not responding.
*   You will lose any unsaved information in this application.
*   Press CTRL+ALT+DELETE to restart your computer. You will
    lose any unsaved information in all applications.

       Press ENTER for OK or ESC to cancel: OK
```

As the message text indicates, you can simply press Enter to close the unresponsive application. By the way, if the application isn't unresponsive, Windows knows this, and the message text indicates as much. In this case, you can press Enter to return to the application.

Patience is a virtue

Before you conclude that an application is ignoring you, consider the possibility that it is busy instead. Some applications may be running macros, for example. Other applications may be printing to a spool file (which gets sent to Print Manager for printing) or may be executing some command you've given.

You Get an Application Error

Sometimes an application asks Windows to do the impossible. When this happens—which isn't very often since the advent of Windows version 3.1, thankfully—Windows displays a message box that says there's been an **application error.**

Close the application

When Windows does alert you to an application error, it usually gives you two choices. You can close the application, or you can ignore the error.

If you've been working with a **document** and have made changes that you haven't yet saved, you can ignore the application error and then save the document. Save the document using a new **filename,** however. You don't want to replace the previous document file with a new corrupted document file. Then close the application.

If you haven't made any changes or haven't made changes you need to save, simply close the application.

QUICK REFERENCE

Any time you explore some exotic location, you're bound to see flora and fauna you can't identify. To make sure you can identify the commands and toolbar buttons you see in Microsoft Windows, the Quick Reference describes these items in systematic detail.

Program Manager Menu Guide

File Menu

New...	Adds groups and program items to Program Manager
Open	Opens the selected group window or starts the application represented by the selected program item
Move...	Moves the selected program item to another group
Copy...	Copies the selected program item to another group
Delete	Removes the selected group or program item
Properties...	Changes a group name or changes a program item name, an icon, an application, and a working directory
Run...	Starts an application or runs a command—as long as you know the path and filename of the application or command
Exit Windows...	Quits Program Manager and closes Windows

Options Menu

Auto Arrange	Turns on and off automatic program item arrangement. When feature is turned on, Windows arranges the program items in a group window whenever you do something that messes up the window—for example, change the window size, add program items, or move program items.
Minimize on Use	Turns on and off the minimize Program Manager feature. When feature is turned on, Windows minimizes Program Manager once you start an application.

Save Settings on Exit	Turns on and off the save Program Manager settings feature. When the feature is turned on, Windows remembers how Program Manager looks when you quit Windows and redisplays Program Manager this same way the next time you start Windows. A boon for nostalgia buffs.

You can tell when an Options menu feature is turned on

Windows places a check mark in front of the Options menu command name when the feature is turned on.

Window Menu

Cascade	Arranges the open windows in a stack, but so that each window's title bar is visible
Tile	Arranges the open windows side by side, in a manner similar to the way ceramic tiles get arranged in a shower or a bath
Arrange Icons	Arranges the group or program items in the active window into neat little rows

About the numbered Window menu commands

The Window menu also lists as numbered commands each of the groups you or Windows has created. You can open a listed group window by choosing the numbered command.

Help Menu

Contents	Lists the major Help topic categories for Program Manager
Search for Help On...	Provides help on a topic you specify
How to Use Help	Lists the major Help topic categories for the Help application
Windows Tutorial	Starts the online tutorial about Windows
About Program Manager...	Displays the Microsoft Windows copyright notice, tells which mode Windows is running in, and gives the available memory and system resources

HELP MENU GUIDE

File Menu

Open...	Opens the Help file you specify
Print Topic	Prints the Help topic showing in the Help application window
Print Setup...	Changes the active Windows printer and its print settings
Exit	Quits the Help application and returns you whence you came

Edit Menu

Copy...	Allows you to copy selected Help file information to the Clipboard
Annotate...	Allows you to add text to the current Help topic and then flags your addition with a paper clip next to the title

Bookmark Menu

Define...	Lets you mark (with a named bookmark) the current Help topic so that you can more easily find the topic later. Also lets you remove old bookmarks you no longer need.

Finding your place

Once you create and name a bookmark using the Bookmark Define command, Help adds the bookmark name to the Bookmark menu. You can quickly move to the bookmark by choosing the bookmark name from the Bookmark menu. By the way, if you create more than nine bookmarks, the menu doesn't have room to display them all. So Help adds a tenth menu command named More. Choose More when you want to see the tenth and any subsequent bookmarks.

Help Menu

How to Use Help	Lists the major Help topic categories for the Help application
Always on Top	Tells Windows to display the Help application window on top of any other application windows—even when Help isn't the foreground application
About Help...	Displays the Microsoft Windows Help copyright notice, tells which mode Windows is running in, and gives the available memory and system resources

Using the Help command buttons

Underneath the Help menu bar are five command buttons: Contents, which lists the major Help topics for the application from which you started Help; Search, which provides help on a topic you specify; Back, which displays the previous Help topic; History, which lists the Help topics you've perused thus far; and either Glossary, which lists all the Windows Help Glossary pop-up definitions, or Index, which lists the Help topics.

PRINT MANAGER MENU GUIDE

View Menu

Time/Date Sent	Turns on and off the print queue's display of the print file creation time and date. (Command is checked when time and date are displayed.)
Print File Size	Turns on and off the print queue's display of the print file size. (Command is checked when feature is on.)
Refresh	Immediately updates the print queue. (Print Manager also automatically updates the print queue periodically.)
Selected Net Queue	Shows the print queue for the network printer you're connected to
Other Net Queue	Shows the print queue for the network printer you're not connected to
Exit	Quits Print Manager and deletes any print files in the print queue

Options Menu

Low Priority	Tells Windows that printing is a low-priority task so that you want it (Windows) to use most of your computer's horsepower for running other applications
Medium Priority	Tells Windows that, hey, printing is just as important as everything else you're doing so that it (Windows) should equally share your computer's horsepower between Print Manager and any other running applications
High Priority	Tells Windows to devote more of your computer's horsepower to printing and less of it to running other applications
Alert Always	Tells Windows that you want to see Print Manager messages (such as "out of paper") even when Print Manager is a background application

Flash If Inactive	Tells Windows that you want the Print Manager title bar or icon to flash on and off, like a neon sign, when Print Manager is running as a background application or as a minimized icon and has an important message for you (such as "out of paper")
Ignore If Inactive	Tells Print Manager that the whole world's got troubles and that you don't want to hear about its (Print Manager's) troubles or read its messages
Network Settings...	Tells Print Manager how it should feel about things when you're using a network printer (such as whether Print Manager or the network should be the one to print)
Network Connections...	Tells Print Manager how it should connect to a network printer
Printer Setup...	Describes the printer you're using with Print Manager

Help Menu

Contents	Lists the major Help topic categories for Print Manager
Search for Help On...	Provides help on a topic you specify
How to Use Help	Lists the major Help topic categories for the Help application
About Print Manager	Displays the Microsoft Windows Print Manager copyright notice, tells which mode Windows is running in, and gives the available memory and system resources

File Manager Menu Guide

File Menu

Open	Opens the selected directory window, starts the selected application, opens the selected document using the application that the document is associated with, or expands the selected directory
Move...	Moves selected files or directories from one directory to another directory
Copy...	Copies selected files or directories
Delete...	Erases selected files or directories
Undelete...	Unerases selected file or files. (This command appears only if you've got MS-DOS version 6 or later.)
Rename...	Changes selected file or directory name
Properties...	Adjusts selected file's attributes
Run...	Starts selected application or opens selected document using the associated application
Print...	Prints selected file using the associated application
Associate...	Tells Windows which application it should open when files with a particular extension are chosen
Create Directory...	Creates a new directory in the active directory
Search...	Looks for files or directories that match a specified description
Select Files...	Selects the files in a directory that match a specified description
Exit	Quits File Manager

Disk Menu

Copy Disk...	Copies a floppy disk
Label Disk...	Adds or renames a disk's volume label
Format Disk...	Formats a floppy disk
Make System Disk...	Copies the MS-DOS operating-system files to a floppy disk so that you can start your computer using the floppy disk
Network Connections...	Connects your computer to or disconnects your computer from a network
Connect Network Drive...	Connects your computer to a network disk drive
Disconnect Network Drive...	Disconnects your computer from a network disk drive
Select Drive...	Changes the active disk

About the network commands

The Network Connections, Connect Network Drive, and Disconnect Network Drive commands don't appear on the Disk menu if your computer isn't connected to a network. That makes sense, right?

Tree Menu

Expand One Level	Shows files and subdirectories in selected, collapsed directory by expanding the directory tree
Expand Branch	Shows all the files, subdirectories, and subdirectory files in the selected, collapsed directory by expanding the directory tree
Expand All	Shows all the files and subdirectories by expanding the directory tree
Collapse Branch	Hides the files and subdirectories in the selected directory by collapsing the directory tree
Indicate Expandable Branches	Shows which directories have subdirectories by placing a plus sign on the directory icon

View Menu

Tree and Directory	Shows the active directory's directory tree and current contents in File Manager's active document, or directory, window
Tree Only	Shows only a directory tree in the active directory window
Directory Only	Shows only the directory contents in the active directory window
Split	Allows you to reposition the bar that splits the active directory window
Name	Tells File Manager to display only file and directory names in the active directory window because you don't want to see any other file information. (File Manager places a check mark in front of this command name if you choose it instead of one of the other two View options: All File Details or Partial Details.)
All File Details	Tells File Manager to tell the whole story, that is, to display each file's name, size in bytes, last modification date and time, and attributes. (File Manager places a check mark in front of this command name if you choose it instead of one of the other two View options: Name or Partial Details.)

Partial Details...	Tells File Manager to display specified file and directory information. (File Manager places a check mark in front of this command name if you choose it instead of one of the other two View options: Name or All File Details.)
Sort by Name	You can guess what this does, right? It simply tells File Manager to sort files and directories in alphabetic order using their filenames.
Sort by Type	Tells File Manager to sort files and directories in alphabetic order using their file extensions. (Because directories usually don't have an extension, they show first in the list.)
Sort by Size	Tells File Manager to sort files in order of size, starting with the largest file
Sort by Date	Tells File Manager to sort files in order of file modification date, starting with the most recently modified file
By File Type...	Tells File Manager to display directories, applications, or files with specified names or extensions

Options Menu

Confirmation...	Alternately tells File Manager that you do or don't want to see confirmation messages
Font...	Specifies which font you want File Manager to use
Status Bar	Alternately tells File Manager that you do or don't want to see the status bar at the bottom of the File Manager application window. (File Manager places a check mark in front of this command name when you've told it you want to see Status Bar.)

continues

Options Menu *(continued)*

Minimize on Use	Tells Windows to minimize File Manager when you start an application from File Manager. (File Manager places a check mark in front of this command name when you've told Windows to do the minimization thing.)
Save Settings on Exit	Tells File Manager that you want its application window and directory windows to look the same the next time you start File Manager as they do when you exit File Manager. (File Manager places a check mark in front of this command name when you've told it you want to save the settings.)

Tools Menu

Backup...	Starts the Microsoft Tools Backup application
Anti-virus...	Starts the Microsoft Tools Anti-Virus application
DoubleSpace Info...	Displays information about a disk you've compressed with the MS-DOS version 6 DoubleSpace utility

About the Tools menu commands

Your copy of File Manager may not have a Tools menu. The Tools menu and its commands really come with MS-DOS versions 6 and later.

Window Menu

New Window	Opens another directory window
Cascade	Arranges the open directory windows in a stack, but so that each window's title bar is visible

Tile	Arranges the open directory windows in a manner similar to the way ceramic tiles get arranged in a shower or a bath
Arrange Icons	Arranges minimized directory windows into neat little rows
Refresh	Updates the list of directories and files shown in the directory window for any file or directory changes

About the numbered Window menu commands

The Window menu also lists as numbered commands each of the directory windows you've opened. You can activate a listed directory window by choosing the numbered command.

Help Menu

Contents	Lists the major Help topic categories for File Manager
Search for Help On...	Provides help on a topic you specify
How to Use Help	Lists the major Help topic categories for the Help application
About File Manager	Displays the Microsoft Windows File Manager copyright notice, tells which mode Windows is running in, and gives the available memory and system resources

CONTROL-PANEL MENU GUIDE

Settings Menu

Color

Changes the colors of windows and dialog boxes

Fonts

Adds and removes TrueType fonts

Ports

Sets the serial communication port options

Mouse

Changes the way your mouse or trackball works

Desktop

Changes the desktop colors and patterns, and lets you add a screen saver

Keyboard

Changes the way your keyboard works

Printers

Installs and removes the printers you'll use with Windows

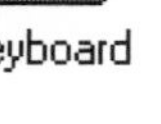
International

Describes which language, currency symbol, and date and time formats Windows should use

Date/Time

Changes your computer's internal calendar date and clock time

 386 Enhanced	Describes how Windows shares communication ports, schedules background and foreground applications, and employs virtual memory when you're running Windows in 386 enhanced mode
 Drivers	Installs and removes any strange or unusual devices you'll use with Windows—for example, sound cards
 Sound	Describes which sounds Windows should make when certain events occur
Exit	Quits Control Panel so that you can get on with your life

If you see more Control-Panel Settings commands

You may see more Control-Panel Settings commands than are listed here. You may have a Settings menu command and an icon for network drivers, for example. Or you may have a Settings menu command and an icon for MIDI drivers.

Help Menu

Contents	Lists the major Help topic categories for Control Panel
Search for Help On...	Provides help on a topic you specify
How to Use Help	Lists the major Help topic categories for the Help application
About Control Panel...	Displays the Microsoft Windows Control Panel copyright notice, tells which mode Windows is running in, and gives the available memory and system resources

SPECIAL CHARACTERS

A

B

C

D

E

F

G

H

I

N

O

R

S

T

U

V

W

The manuscript for this book was prepared and submitted to Microsoft Press in electronic form. Text files were prepared using Microsoft Word 2.0 for Windows. Pages were composed by Stephen L. Nelson, Inc., using PageMaker 5.0 for Windows, with text in Minion and display type in Copperplate. Composed pages were delivered to the printer as electronic prepress files.

Cover Designer
Rebecca Geisler

Cover Illustrator
Eldon Doty

Interior Text Designer
The Understanding Business

Page Layout and Typography
Greg Schultz

Editor
Pat Coleman

Technical Editor
Clay Martin

Indexer
Julie Kawabata

Printed on recycled paper stock.

INFORMATION FROM THE SOURCE

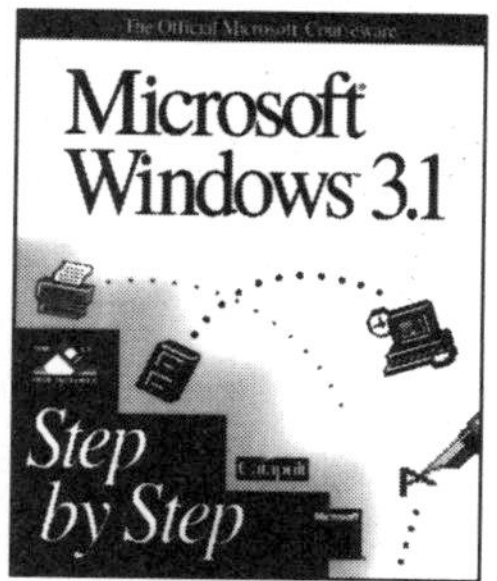

Microsoft® Windows™ 3.1 Step by Step

Catapult, Inc.

The fastest way to learn Windows 3.1! Complete with follow-along lessons and disk-based practice files, it includes scores of real-world business examples. Ideal for business, classroom, and home use.

296 pages, softcover with one 3.5-inch disk
$29.95 ($39.95 Canada) ISBN 1-55615-501-8

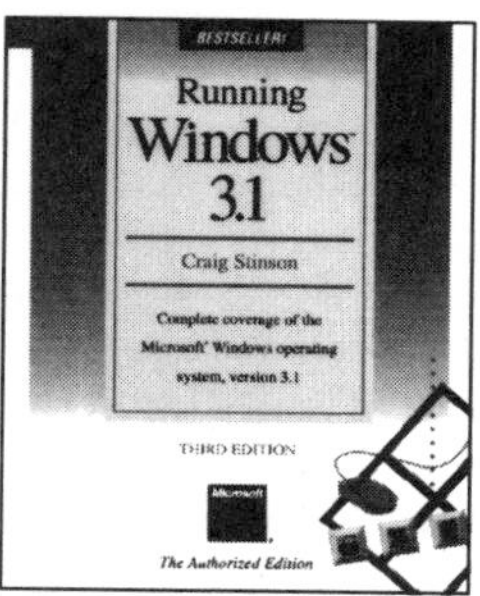

Running Windows™ 3.1

Craig Stinson

"The text is clear and concise. Its detailed explanations will save you much more time than it takes to read it." **PC Magazine**

This Microsoft-authorized guide to Windows 3.1 clearly delves into the whys and hows of every feature of Windows, with supporting examples.

560 pages, softcover $27.95 ($37.95 Canada)
ISBN 1-55615-373-2

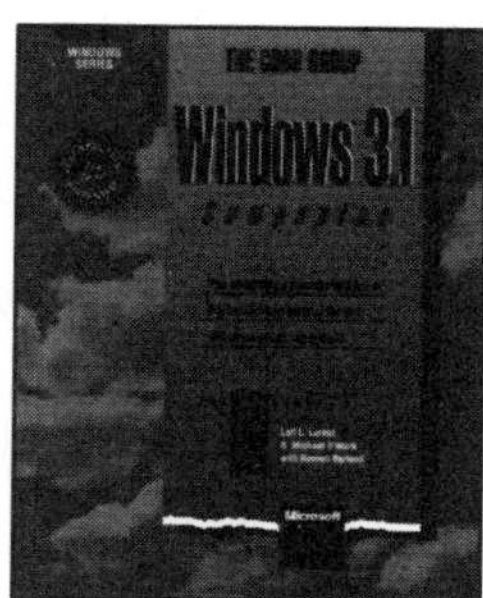

Windows™ 3.1 Companion

The Cobb Group

"Covers the basics thoroughly.... An excellent reference." **PC Magazine**

A completely updated edition of the best-selling tutorial from the Cobb Group, written in the clear and conversational style that is their trademark. Packed with step-by-step tutorials, great examples, and expert advice.

544 pages, softcover $27.95 ($37.95 Canada)
ISBN 1-55615-372-4

Microsoft Press

Microsoft Press® books are available wherever quality books are sold and through CompuServe's Electronic Mall—GO MSP. Call 1-800-MSPRESS for direct ordering information or for placing credit card orders.* Please refer to BBK when placing your order. Prices subject to change.

*In Canada, contact Macmillan Canada, Attn: Microsoft Press Dept., 164 Commander Blvd., Agincourt, Ontario, Canada M1S 3C7, or call (416) 293-8464, ext. 340.

Outside the U.S. and Canada, write to International Coordinator, Microsoft Press, One Microsoft Way, Redmond, WA 98052-6399.